The Cruise of *Naromis*

August in the Baltic 1939

About this book: Editor's note

I was wedged in a corner of the attic, looking for something else completely, when I came across my father's account of his cruise on board *Naromis*. With a slight shock I remember him trying to tell me – or us – about his passage through the Kiel Canal on the eve of the Second World War, then giving up when he saw that I, at least, didn't understand the significance at all. Until this unexpected find I had also failed to realise that he had written up his experiences, assembled as many of his photographs as he was able and prepared the book for possible publication. And that all this had been done when he was serving in the Royal Navy, thousands of miles from home.

I am George Jones's daughter and I am honoured to be his editor and publisher. I sat for a long while behind the barricade of boxes in the cluttered, dusty attic reading with tears in my eyes. Not because the material is distressing, it isn't. This is an ordinary summer's cruise undertaken at an extraordinary time. I felt emotional because I caught glimpses of the person I had loved, mainly in his receptiveness to beauty and his passion for small boats, and I realised how little I knew of his life before we met.

My father died in 1983 aged sixty-five, suddenly, of a heart attack. He had met the first three of his grandchildren (briefly) but not the other six. He has been dead now for longer than I knew him during the time that our lives overlapped. I decided at once to give this cruise to all the family as a simple Christmas booklet. That it has become something more is largely due to my partner Francis Wheen, who was astonished at my cluelessness at not having noticed its interest as a historic document, and to my friend Captain Richard Woodman, who described it as "delightful" and asked to be put down for a copy.

Then I found another two suitcases retrieved from under the eaves of my mother's former cottage. There were some diaries, poems, scrapbooks and a file marked "GAJ Navy". I knew that I knew nothing about Dad's time in the war. Because he was an administrator not a hero I had assumed it was uninteresting. I don't now think so.

One thing Dad cared about was presentation. He was interested in matters such as printers' fonts and I think he would approve the care and expertise that this book's typesetter, Megan Trudell, has put into her selection. I know he would have bonded immediately with Claudia Myatt who has drawn the map of the voyage and supplied a Pierhead Painter's impression of *Naromis* setting out on her adventure. Claudia was for a while the secretary of the East Anglian Group of Marine Artists, which Dad and his friends had founded in the 1970s and she shares to the full his feeling for wooden boats and the effects of light reflecting off river water. My contribution is the two essays either side of the Cruise, written from the contents of those suitcases.

I would like to thank Colin Davis, owner of MY *Seren* and archivist of the Thames Vintage Boat Club, for permission to reproduce *Naromis*'s lines from his site and also for the information both from him and from Colin West about her later life. Thanks too to Ian Stewart, archivist of the Little Ship Club. I am indebted to H.T. Lenton & J.J. Colledge's *Warships of World War II* (Ian Allen 1964) and to all the people who maintain detailed information about ships and people on the internet. I have also used Corelli Barnett's *Engage the Enemy More Closely* (Penguin 1990), Richard Woodman's *The Real Cruel Sea: The Merchant Navy in the Battle of the Atlantic, 1939-1943* (John Murray 2005) and J.P. Foynes's *The Battle of the East Coast 1939-1945* (published by the author 1994).

Julia Jones, December 2016

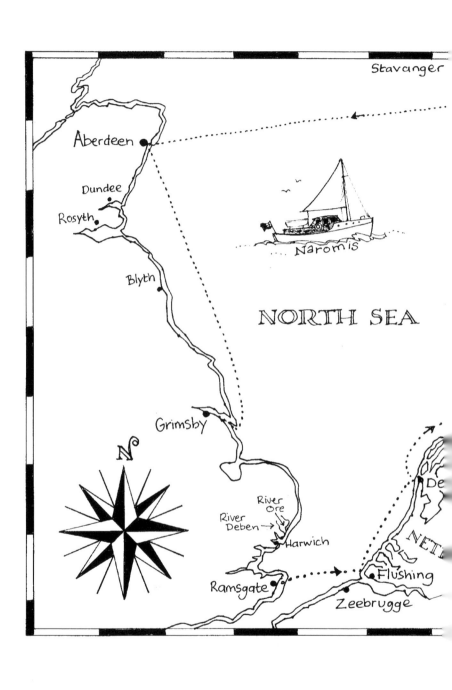

Stavanger

Aberdeen

Dundee

Rosyth

Blyth

NORTH SEA

Naromis

Grimsby

N

River Ore

River Deben

Harwich

De

NET

Flushing

Ramsgate

Zeebrugge

Farsund
Kristiansand
SKAGGERAK
The Skaw
KATTEGAT
Gothenburg
SWEDEN
DENMARK
Elsinore
Copenhagen
Malmo
Nakskov
Orehoved
BALTIC
Heligoland Bight
Kiel
Laboé
Cuxhaven
Danzig
GERMANY
NDS

This book is for Jack, Frank, Georgeanna, George, Ruth,
Twinkie, Bertie, Archie & Louisa

First published in 2017 by Golden Duck UK Ltd
Sokens, Green Steet, Pleshey, nr Chelmsford, Essex CM3 1HT
www.golden-duck.co.uk

G.A. Jones photos ©Julia, Nicholas & Edward Jones
Cover illustration & map © Claudia Myatt 2017
Naromis lines (design drawing) © Colin Davis MY *Seren*
MY *Bayeed* in Gibralter (photograph) © Colin West

Design by Megan Trudell
emdashtype.uk
Ebook conversion by Matti Gardner
matti@grammaticus.co.uk

Printed and bound in the UK by 4edge Ltd Hockley

The Cruise of *Naromis:*
August in the Baltic 1939

G.A. Jones

Edited and with additional material
by Julia Jones

GOLDEN DUCK

Contents

George Jones in 1938 aged 20

A Coming of Age

GEORGE AUBREY JONES was born on 5 January 1918 in Fornham All Saints, near Bury St Edmunds in Suffolk. On 4 January 1939 he was living in the West Midlands and was about to be twenty-one.

I write the following at 11.30 pm.

This is the last thing I shall write while I am still a legal infant. I am very sad about it but time is inexorable. Outside a keen wind is trying to get into my bedroom – the old North Room. Everything outside is white in the moonlight and snow. The beauty from Grace's window overlooking the lake is saddening. For tomorrow it will pass on as surely I as pass on from twenty to twenty-one. There are no more milestones for me to pass. Away with melancholy! Everyone is very kind and I have spent an admirable evening saying nothing. Mr Lewis made some excellent black coffee and I have been eating crème de menthe – the sweetmeat par excellence. I nearly ruined the whole tin by warming them by the fire and forgetting. I am getting delightfully forgetful nowadays – a sign, I hope, of later genius.

I go to bed tonight with the picture of Kirton Creek by Bertram Priestman on my right, an artificial red rose and Jute's rubber doll – specially requisitioned by Grace for the occasion. I had thought of crossing the threshold in the chapel yard, but it is bitter cold so I would not to be able to think. I am wondering tonight whether the arrows will be flying in the frontiers before the snow is gone from the mountains.

George kept his diary throughout 1939 until he set off in August for *Naromis* and the Baltic. The significance of the red rose and the borrowed doll are lost but the watercolour of Kirton Creek was an inspired choice to place beside his bed that night. Kirton Creek is a tributary of the River Deben in Suffolk, the river George had loved since he was a young child and which he would continue to love throughout his life. Ramsholt Church, where he is buried, looks directly across the river to Kirton Creek.

River Deben at Ramsholt in 1938

After the Munich Crisis of 1938 many people approached 1939 with a sense of apprehension. When George began to imagine "arrows flying in the frontiers" he decided to stop writing his diary and spend the last moments of his "infancy" reading W.E. Henley. He would surely have included Henley's "Invictus" in this night of private vigil.

> Out of the night that covers me,
> Black as the pit from pole to pole,
> I thank whatever gods may be
> For my unconquerable soul.
>
> In the fell clutch of circumstance
> I have not winced nor cried aloud.
> Under the bludgeoning of chance
> My head is bloody, but unbowed.

> Beyond this place of wrath and tears
> Looms but the Horror of the shade,
> And yet the menace of the years
> Finds, and shall find me, unafraid.
>
> It matters not how strait the gate,
> How charged with punishments the scroll,
> I am the master of my fate:
> I am the captain of my soul.

He might then have added, "I wish…" George's 1939 diary is a painfully truthful document. Like many people in their early twenties he was uncertain who he was or what he might become. He was occasionally pretentious, privately ambitious, regularly self-doubting. He realised he was self-centred and feared he might become "a bore". George loved the beauty of the English countryside and was particularly responsive to the effects of light – even on the chimney pots of Edgbaston. He also loved poetry, music, architecture and was often intensely spiritual. He drank too much and did a lot of "kissing". He was afraid of being afraid.

The "old North Room" where George slept that January night was in Grafton Manor house, an impressive early Tudor building near Bromsgrove in Worcestershire. There was indeed a lake, a chapel, a tithe barn, an atmospheric chapel yard, all in twenty acres of land. The manor site pre-dates the Norman Conquest and its history is redolent with the names and titles of aristocratic families, people who might have taken their significance for granted. George however was a tenant farmer's son from Suffolk, living in lodgings in Birmingham, completing his three years as an articled clerk and dealing on the city's Stock Exchange. The people with whom he was staying were not grandees and had bought the manor at Depression prices.

George's father had died as the result of an accident in 1933 when George was fourteen. The period of poverty and uncertainty that followed his father's death left a permanent impression. George, who was the youngest of three brothers, had to leave school and go to work: in a paint factory for £1 a week and then in Woolworth's for 25 shillings. In 1934 he had also spent a short period as a barge boy. Materially the 1930s were a difficult time for many people yet George seems also to have lacked emotional security. He was for ever grateful to two of his aunts, the Misses George-Anna and Margaret Aubrey-Jones, for rescuing him from drudgery and giving him a home. "The Aunts" owned a girls' boarding school in Felixstowe in Suffolk – near the mouth of his beloved River Deben. They took him in, assumed responsibility for his well-being and sent him back to Ipswich School to finish his education.

George grew tall and lanky in his later teens though he was neither of those things as an adult. He had poor eyesight ("the worst astigmatism in East Suffolk" he used to claim) and had suffered rheumatic fever as a child. Nevertheless he played hockey in the school first XI and was a member of the athletics team. He had learned to sail from Felixstowe beach in 1925 and migrated up river to Waldringfield when his father built a hut there in 1928 in a disused coprolite pit. He owned a dinghy – probably with his brother Jack – and relished listening to the "owd boys" of the river and cadging brief trips on coasters and barges. There was still coal coming up the River Deben in those days. He was probably clever and hard-working and recollected his time at Ipswich School with some fondness. He was a day boy with plenty of opportunity to make friends with girls.

George also seems to have had some quality that brought out a protective instinct in older women. Grace, the mistress of Grafton, who had procured the odd-sounding "rubber doll" for this last night of his legal childhood, was a distant cousin. She was unfailingly generous towards him and told him he was named in her Will as the inheritor of Grafton – after her son, Peter, her daughter, Betty, and their as yet unborn children. According to his diary the Mrs Lewis who made such good black coffee "wants to adopt me". Earlier in the evening he records that he had sat "against her knees". Another older woman, Mrs Brockenhurst, also made offers of "adoption". She played music and read poetry to him, shared her personal memories of Elgar and held out hopes of employment with her friend Sir Barry Jackson, founder of the Birmingham Repertory Company and the Malvern Festival. And there were more Aunts, five of them, married and unmarried, living at or near the family farm at Newney Green in Essex. But the two that remained special for all of George's life were Georgie and Margaret at Fleet House.

When his mother, Edith, had parted with the last of their father's holdings for a knock down price in 1937, George and his brothers were angry and upset. Although George was the youngest and had no interest in farming this event may have affected him the most deeply. His oldest brother Hugh was already married and had a child: Jack, the middle brother, remained particularly close to their mother – her "mouthpiece" George called him. Jack was also living in Birmingham and Edith lived with him. It was George who was somehow, indefinably, rootless. "And so goes our last straw," he wrote when he heard she had left the farm. Then, a few weeks later, when he believed (mistakenly) that he was no longer welcome at Grafton, he took immediate refuge in Felixstowe. "What I shall do when Georgie and Margaret go, I don't know. They are marvellous and they are standing by me." (28 September 1938)

It was at Fleet House School that he had met Betty Murray-Willis, a distant cousin who was working there temporarily. She was five years older than he was and they became friends for life. Betty's father Alfred (always known as Murray) was a Birmingham stockbroker. He had been bankrupt but was continuing to trade. George was quick with figures so, when he had passed his Matriculation exams in 1936 and left school, he was articled to H.C. Willis & Son and moved from

Suffolk to the West Midlands. Grace Murray-Willis had recently bought Grafton Manor and she immediately made George welcome. Though he had a room in Edgbaston he was so often at Grafton that he wrote it as his alternative address – in his diary at least. George loved the beauty of the manor, particularly the chapel yard, and also the easy social life in which he was automatically included. He was glad to help by mowing the lawns, hoeing the paths, weeding the flower beds, painting the punt on the lake. He was almost one of the family – but not quite. When the question of a partnership in the firm came up, it was obvious that this would go to Peter Murray-Willis, a keen Worcestershire county cricketer, rather than George Jones, the industrious employee.

Grafton Manor

The morning of his twenty-first birthday finally arrived on 5 January and George was "relieved" to find that he felt no different than he had on 4 January. Murray-Willis took him out to lunch, then he set off for Essex to stay with his oldest brother Hugh and his wife Louise who were living near Colchester. Their mother was also there, briefly, and they ate fried plaice together. Late that afternoon George took himself across to Mersea Island.

As I passed over the Strood I gazed for minutes towards the East and listened to the terns and peewits on the mud. Then towards the golden sun, glimmering on the still water that thinly covered the mud. The mud itself was golden and faintly warm. Then to the Beach: two barges were dreaming out on the tideway and the Blackwater was quietly taking them to the sea. There was not a breath of wind, the sun got redder over Cobmarsh and finally set in a pillow of night clouds. (6 January 1939)

After donning a white waistcoat, drinking too much and dancing "the dance of the inebriates" George sobered up, visited any number of aunts, was suitably impressed by his 21-candle birthday cake and was back in the H.C. Willis office on Monday morning. In the evening he wrote a poem, then, on the following day, he sent four short poems "in hopelessness" to Alberta Vickridge, editor of the *Jongleur*.

The *Jongleur* was a quarterly magazine of neo-Georgian romantic verse. It ran from 1927-1956 and was hand-printed for much of its existence. In its heyday the *Jongleur* attracted poems from all over Britain and George was rightly delighted when he heard, a fortnight later, that Alberta had accepted one of his poems ("the one I like least") for publication; "Among such giants as Wilfred Gibson!" (24 January 1939) He had been reading, writing and studying poetry in his spare time, together with music, art, architecture and literature. He took his writing seriously and this acceptance was his first success. By the time his copy arrived in March, however, his triumph had evaporated: "It was the spirit of ages ago that wrote this poem and has no connection with this be-bowlered stockbroker." (8 March 1939)

George, aged 21, was dealing on the Birmingham Stock Exchange. His dealer's commission was his livelihood and he had his clients' interests to consider as well as his responsibility to H.C. Willis & Son. "I do not know why I always mention the markets," he wrote in his diary, "It means so little and is forgotten as soon as it is closed" (17 February 1939) yet he continued recording prices through January, February, March and April. George was caught up in the thrill of profit-making, buoyed up by his successes and cast down by his successes and failures. These were volatile months as the markets waited on Hitler's speeches or responded to Wall Street jitters or to Chamberlain's efforts for peace. In 1938 George had read *Mein Kampf* as part of his self-education, now he watched as the progress of Nazism sent prices tumbling.

Monday 13th March 1939: Mexican Eagles + 1/6. Up to 9/6 bid before official opening! We buy 2550 and sell 100. Markets a bit depressed on news of Slovakia. I am a mild bear. Sell Palmers and Nikvits [?] like a damn fool! However bears will be bears!

Tuesday: An ill-fated day because I buy 100 Amal. Bauhits [?] The finest moments were those just before retiring. The lights were low and I smoked just one cigarette. At last I felt alone with myself.

Wednesday: Czecho-Slovakia non est! The beginning of the fall. Bought Steels at 67. Two and a half points down in an hour! Slump in street due to Hitler marching into Slovakia. Phones out of order so was unable to cut loss.

Thursday 16th: The debacle continues, prices slumping severally. Hitler in Prague. Hungary in Ruthenia.

Friday 17th March: I am not likely to forget today in a hurry. I lost £15 in one fell swoop and had to close. Indeed Black Friday with rumours and counter rumours. Chamberlain makes a fighting speech in Birmingham Town Hall, broadcast to the world.

The Prime Minister, speaking in his native city, again defended his actions at Munich but he condemned Hitler for breaking his word on Czechoslovakia and pledged to resist any further territorial expansion by Germany. As well as reiterating his relief that the country had not already gone to war, he gave some hint what Britain's future policy of intransigence in the defence of liberty could mean to every individual. "The Government, as always, must bear the main responsibility, but I know that all individuals will wish to review their own position, too, and to consider again if they have done all they can to offer their service to the State."

As a twenty-one year old George must have known that his was the generation most likely to be required to offer their service directly. Throughout these early months of 1939 the question of war obtrudes into his diary and never arouses anything other than dread. George was not a macho young man: on a family shoot earlier in the year he records that he "shot into the air as my contribution to the day's sport." Anthony Eden had held a National Service rally in Birmingham in February. "'We'll go,' says Murray. Instead we go to the Midland and get delightfully drunk." (21 February 1939) Alcohol was an obvious escape from strain.

Wednesday 22nd March: Another slump – vague and unfounded rumours send the prices nose-diving again. Murray and I are desperately worried. Tomorrow settlement day.

Thursday 23rd: Upward movement again. Cannot understand the psychology of the market. There is no good news and yet there is recovery. Murray terribly canned tonight – quite balmy.

George was also drinking too much. He found himself uncomfortably caught up in false excuses to Grace for her husband's late and drunken returns or an unwilling spectator at marital disharmony. He began to avoid her and to see himself as a split personality – too often as a "Mr Hyde" behaving badly. He longed for his other self, "Dr Jekyll and his poems", but felt trapped. When one of his female confidantes accused him of "losing his individuality, his enthusiasm and becoming ordinary," he tried to excuse himself by explaining "that I had grown up and out of my boyish enthusiasms, into steadfast ambition" but he knew this was not true: "It is the active markets and Mr Hyde that have throttled me". (28 March 1939)

Weekends bought escape of a different type. George and his brother Jack, who was working as an industrial designer and drawing boats as his private passion, were both members of the newly formed Severn Sailing Club. They sailed on the Severn from Tewkesbury to Worcester and on the Avon up to Pershore. This offered opportunities, if becalmed, to leave the boats and walk up beautiful Bredon Hill with its panoramic views across the western counties. In the early spring of 1939 there was fitting-out to be done at weekends and, by the end of March, George had his dinghy, *Sea Spray*, back on the water:

It is blowing half a gale but I closely reef "Spray" and we hurtle down the Avon with great waves washing the banks. There were a great many swans which rose off the water with a whirring of wings and a paddling of feet. Also a tern, peewits, mallard and teal. Lock through at Tewkesbury. (26 March 1939)

Before the Start: Worcester to Tewkesbury, Severn Sailing Club

It must have been hugely depressing to return to work the following morning to news of trouble in the Polish Corridor and another week of falling markets. "The veil of war is heavy over us." (27 March 1939)

George also had a boat in Suffolk. This was *Hustler*, a sixteen-foot open boat built in 1881, later extended to eighteen feet and for many years the fastest boat on the Deben. By mid-April 1939 *Hustler* too was back in commission and sailing "magnificently". Many people, during this last summer before the war, articulated and indulged their emotional relationship with the landscape of England (and doubtless Scotland and Wales as well). Back in Birmingham, George and his mother spent a rare day together climbing the Clent Hills up to the four stones, looking out over Wales and smelling the sea. (15 April 1939)

Grafton too was glorious:

Shall I forget lying on a mattress gulping in the hot sun and looking up at the tall chimneys of Grafton against an incredibly dark blue sky? Listening to the stillness with the hum of a bee toiling over the lawn and the sweet smell of cut grass. The world was quiet, its armies were silent and time stood still. (18 April 1939)

Except that time did not stand still and the armies continued to muster. George had a long talk with his Aunt Georgie and told her that he was "not progressing in any direction". (22 April 1939) His soul-searching convinced him that "I seem to have lost all idea of beauty, to have become ordinary, self-centred, aimless, completely static, unable to live, write, love or even work. I pray God help me to regain myself." (25 April 1939) By now he was explicitly worried about his mental health: "I talk witlessly of the things I hear other people say and of the ideas I had and formed a year ago."

Budget Day, 25 April, saw him retreating to one of his most reliable sources of comfort, the Birmingham Oratory. He watched the candles and the everlasting lamps and the gleam of the sun on the wall from the west. On 26 April Neville Chamberlain's government announced a bill introducing conscription for all males aged twenty and twenty-one. By the following day George had made his decision not to wait but to volunteer.

Thursday 27th April 1939: I determine to go to Bristol to try to get a commission or anything in the RNVR – but [car] has a puncture. The markets are at a standstill awaiting Hitler's speech tomorrow, in fact the only thing that is actively dealt in is Rumour Deferred.

In the evening I walked. The pavements were wet from a shower and the air smelt of spring. The evening sky was clear and everything was peaceful and rather sombre. It seemed the eve of doom. Across Edgbaston came the bells of the Old Church rising and falling, now hidden by a house, now clear and tumbling over each other. In the sky there was a plane curling and diving. It seemed synonymous. Here were two things – the culture we loved and believed and the death that perhaps awaited us. Already we were leading a different life amongst the recruiting offices.

Thrushes sang as I walked and they made me melancholic. They sang to me of the days when I was a child and put to bed at six on summer evenings, and of how Mother and Dad used to walk out on the farm at Fornham; and I would wonder whether they would come back to me. I prayed to God that they would not leave me. Everything that I have loved rises up in the memory and I cling to it and kiss it and then turn to prepare for the new life of death that is forced upon me.

By Saturday his car had been repaired and he set off for Bristol. He missed the Commanding Officer but discovered that the officer in charge was a Suffolk man, born not far from Ipswich and well acquainted with the River Deben. George was allowed to go all over the drill ship HMS *Flying Fox* and to "fondle" her six inch guns. He had made his commitment but remained uncertain whether he would be accepted into the RNVR as the Admiralty "do not want yachtsmen with defective eyesight". (11 February 1939) A few days later the acceptance criteria for the RNVSR (Royal Naval Volunteer Supplementary Reserve) for yachtsmen, which had been created in 1937, were extended to include volunteers for an Accountancy branch. George was elated: "The Admiralty creates a Special Reserve for me!" (4 May 1939) He completed his application form the following day, collected suitable testimonials the day after and was taken by a friend, Captain Smith-Masters, to a weekend of lectures at the Bonar Law Memorial College in Ashridge House, Hertfordshire.

On the first evening George stood up at the end of the lecture and asked Admiral of the Fleet Lord Chatfield, Minister for the Coordination of Defence, "Why it is not deemed necessary to establish a naval base on the East Coast between Chatham and Invergordon taking into consideration that at the present time Germany is considered our potential enemy?" But he couldn't afterwards remember what the Admiral said in reply. "I lost his lengthy reply in the reaction from stage-fright. When I got up my throat contracted, my heart nearly bounded out of my chest to see a hundred eyes turned on me." Ashridge was the Conservative Staff College and George made the most of the opportunity to meet the other eminent speakers and get involved in discussions. He also enjoyed lying in the grass to the sound of a distant cricket match and talking to Margaret Smith-Masters about "kissing, horses and motor-cycles".

George had occasionally thought about getting involved in politics (as an alternative to being a "market operator, a writer or a bargee") but "how can I hope to trust myself to guide my country when I cannot at the moment guide my life?" (7 May 1939) He was formally interviewed at HMS *Flying Fox* at the end of June and, finally, on 5th July he learned that he was a "Probationary Temporary Paymaster Sub Lieutenant RNVSR". "I tell everybody that I am an officer – though nothing about the probationary, temporary part." (6 July 1939)

The tone of George's diary had become happier. Earlier in the year he had admitted to himself that courage was "the commodity I lack most in the world". Once he had visited Bristol and volunteered, he seems to have gained confidence. The writer and the sailor in him were allowed to push the stockbroker into the background and there was at least as much in his diary about his adventures with *Hustler* in Suffolk as there was about the movement of prices on the Birmingham Exchange.

George and his sister-in-law Lou (and her dog) spent a particularly memorable weekend in late May sailing from the River Deben to the Ore, then sleeping at Boyton Dock on dew-soaked floor boards. (27 May 1939) In the morning they ate eggs and bacon in Orford, lolled in the sun at Shingle Street, then experienced a tumultuous re-entry to the Deben with a fresh breeze astern: "Yawing and lifting in an alarming manner. The Bar was in a state of turmoil and frankly I had never come through a worse sea." They called on aunts Georgie and Margaret at Fleet House, spent too long in their lovely garden then endured a "miserable" beat up-river to Waldringfield late at night against the ebb. The hut that George's father had built to support his two younger sons' love of sailing was a welcome refuge.

The hut at Waldringfield

George put off returning to Birmingham and the office. Instead he spent an extra day on the Deben down river at Ramsholt listening to George Collins, a previous owner of *Hustler*, talk "long and lovingly" about her. "He used to earn a pound or twenty-five shillings a night trawling from her. We must get a small eight-foot beam-trawl." (29 May 1939) A week later sister-in-law Lou wrote to say that she had found one in West Mersea and was having it repaired. Back in Birmingham George sent more poems to the *Jongleur* and a spate of short articles to the *Birmingham Post*, the *East Anglian Magazine* and the *Yachting Monthly*. Two articles were accepted and even the rejection was encouraging. George began to dream of abandoning stockbroking for the literary life.

He took a week's holiday and stayed in the hut. It was hard to ignore the activity from the A&AEE (Aeroplane and Armament Experimental Establishment) at nearby Martlesham and George heard rumours that there was a boom across the harbour at Harwich and mines already laid. He noted there was "trouble in Tientsin with Japan" and the markets looked "rotten". He read the papers every day but was more interested in the comings and goings of friends, pints in the "Bush" and learning to trawl from *Hustler*. On the final evening he and Lou had "a wonderful sailing-row against the tide" down river from Waldringfield to the Rocks after a day of rain.

The sun broke through for about ten minutes and the lazy grey water was dappled with a path of blood. It was an evening to love with a vague mist hanging over everything and the air sweet with all the rain. The river smelt of saltwater and weed. Our first drag was excellent – three flat fish and about twelve bull-norts [?]. We took the net ashore to unravel it and tried another drag – only four bull-norts so feeling desperately tired, we sailed for home. (16 June 1939)

And so the summer slipped by, mainly at work in Birmingham or in the company of friends, either at Grafton, on the Severn or in

Suffolk at Waldringfield or with The Aunts. It was a high point when the *Yachting Monthly* accepted his brief article about Boyton Dock and offered to pay him 5/-. His brother Jack had already had two of his designs accepted by Maurice Griffiths, the magazine's editor, and there was an undercurrent of competitiveness as well as mutual support between the brothers. George had hopes of spending three days on a destroyer in August as part of his RNVSR training but, on 1st August "Crocker suggests I go to Danzig and pay 9 gns."

Danzig (Gdansk) was a United Nations Free City, created after the Treaty of Versailles. It separated Germany from East Prussia and gave Poland a corridor to the Baltic. In the autumn of 1938 Germany's foreign minister demanded the incorporation of Danzig into the Reich. After the invasion of Czechoslovakia in March 1939, Neville Chamberlain pledged Britain's support for France in the event of a German attack on Poland and George noted in his diary that there "seems to be accruing trouble in the Polish Corridor". (27.3.1939) Tensions in Danzig continued to mount throughout July and August and it was a German battleship moored off the "Free City" that fired the first shots of the invasion on September 1st 1939. An odd destination for a pleasure cruise?

George made his preparations in a hurry. He didn't know any of his future shipmates and details of their intentions are tantalisingly absent. It seems almost certain that "Crocker", who made the original suggestion, was Lieutenant Commander W.S. Crocker who had volunteered for the RNVSR in 1937 and was an active member of the London Division. As no official training was provided for the RNVSR many members formed themselves into Flotillas to organise this for themselves. RNVSR training in London was provided by the Little Ship Club – where *Naromis*'s designer, Higley Halliday, was a member. The Little Ship Club is in the City, an easy walk from Leadenhall Street where *Naromis*'s owner, Mr R.J. Clutton, worked for Schröders. George paid his nine guineas and signed on.

Friday 4th August: Going to Baltic. Hear from Fuller KC.

Fuller KC was "Bill" the trip's navigator, William Archibald Fuller, a barrister with chambers in the Temple. He, like Crocker, was a RNVSR London Division member. R.J. Clutton was not a member but had served in the First World War and was eager to do his bit. Small boat handling was felt to be a potentially important skill and motor cruisers like *Naromis* had already been used for RNVSR training exercises on the Thames. Was this cruise in any sense official reconnaissance or had Clutton simply decided to run across and take a look at Danzig for himself, using RNVSR enthusiasm to man his yacht? George sounded briefly uncertain.

Tuesday 8th: Preparations for Baltic trip. The boat is a 45 ft diesel ship. I don't see that I am going to be much use to them. However.

Wednesday 9th: A wild scurry to get passport signed and photographs.

Thursday: I leave today for London Town, very laden. It is pelting with rain. I have just seen a little Austin 7 toiling up the hill with a boat on top painted battleship grey. Surely this is the spirit of England!

And with that George's 1939 diary reaches its end.

George sailing Hustler, *the boat he left behind*

The Cruise of "NAROMIS"

August in the Baltic 1939

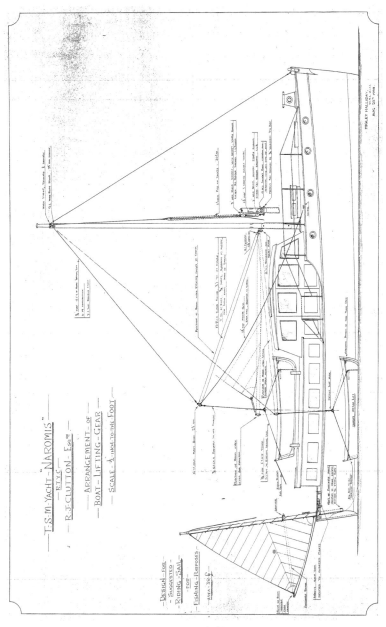

Naromis *lines*

28

Preface

THE OPPORTUNITY for writing up our Baltic trip did not occur until nearly two years after it had taken place. This was when my ship moved out to a foreign station after spending the first part of the war in home waters and I found that life had taken a more favourable slant. So I started with the help of some notes and a well-seasoned memory.

The cruise was quite a short one only lasting three weeks. It was packed with interest especially as the ground covered took us to many areas our Naval forces would operate in during the forthcoming war. It was as though I had been conducted through the scene of a great drama and just managed to get off the stage before the curtain went up!

"NAROMIS" is a 37' twin engine motor cruiser. She was designed by Mr Higley Halliday for Mr R.J. Clutton and built on the Broads in 1938. Throughout the cruise the little ship behaved magnificently, a credit to her designer. She carried a reasonable spread of canvas, enough I think to warrant the designation "sixty-forty" cruiser, if there is such a term. The Dorman diesels also behaved in a praiseworthy manner carrying us hundreds of miles without trouble at a time when a breakdown might have been embarrassing.

Lastly a word of gratitude to Mr Clutton – the owner, skipper and staff officer of the trip. It was a fine achievement to plan and carry into effect the cruise into Germany at a time so uncertain and pregnant with hazard. The original plans had to be recast half way through yet everything worked smoothly and ended well. Altogether we covered thirteen hundred nautical miles and visited half a dozen countries in three weeks.

HMS *FORTH*   G.A.J.

Chapter One: The Beginning

Friday 11th August 1939

THE STOCK EXCHANGE was just about closing for the weekend that Friday afternoon in August as I turned down into Walbrook towards Cannon Street Station. I must have been a strange sight with my yellow oilskins and red sea-boots and many a respectable broker's clerk may have felt mildly shaken. Yesterday I too had been a stockbroker's clerk and had just completed my three year's articles. Today I had put shares aside (for a few weeks, as I thought) and was on my way to help take a yacht to the Baltic... A yacht to the Baltic! – exciting words and something I had always wanted to do. British yachtsmen did not go to that delightful cruising area as often as one would expect and for me, it was breaking fresh ground.

I met Skipper on the train to Ramsgate and later, when we reached the Royal Temple Yacht Club, the rest of the crew were ready for us, the last of the stores on board and everything shipshape. It was a supreme moment this, sitting out on the veranda of the yacht club smoking a pipe with a last glass of English beer within reach, watching the lights, the bustle of the holiday crowds. How we should have appreciated that noisy press of Londoners and those piercing lights had we known it was the last time we should see these things in England for years. Out in the harbour the black shapes of the boats stirred restlessly to the gentle swell that came in through the pier heads. Beyond all this was the sparkling anticipation of the morning to come.

Skips (himself a City banker) had got together a black-coated crew. Bill, the navigator, was a barrister in the Temple. Mike was a medical student and there was Jock, a stockbroker, christened

"Fattie" from the start. He was a wonderful person, large and always roaring with laughter.

Saturday 12th August 1939
WE LEFT next day at 0915. The morning was perfect for making a passage with sunshine after many weeks of cloud and rain. The log was streamed at the North Goodwin L.V. and we laid a course E.S.E at a steady seven knots. This speed was maintained quite easily in a slight sea and following breeze. The day passed in the usual rather monotonous way of sea passages. Interest is confined to the next meal, the log dial and finding a comfortable place to get your head down on the upper deck. My admiration for seamen like Gerbault is unbounded but I am not personally persuaded that there is very great enjoyment in sea passages. The whole joy of "messing around in boats" to my mind, is confined to the boats themselves, the places you go to, the people you meet. There's the joy of getting the best out of your boat, the excitement of a fight to windward, the contentment of warm summer days trimming your sheets to catspaws and trawling for soles along the edge of the mud. There are frosty nights on the saltings, waiting for the ducks, and then on to the sea itself. In small doses it is the only thing: in large brimfuls it loses all its charm and becomes an old bore.

The West Hinder was abeam at 1405, the log recording 34 ½ miles. A tug was streaming off the stern of the light vessel, probably swinging compasses. Two hours later the Wandelaar was sighted to starboard and "NAROMIS" was on a course of 100°. Presently we sighted the Belgium coast and by 1800 we were off Zeebrugge working up against the tide. It was late evening when we reached the Scheldt. Ships were streaming down on the ebb; three Germans in a line, a Swede, a Finn, a Norwegian, an Irishman, an Italian, a Russian and so on. All the way to Flushing we only met a single British ship, an Ellerman "City" boat. This and the "ARANDORA STAR" at Copenhagen were the only two British ships we met during our entire cruise. Although our continental trade is not large this seemed, more than anything, a sign of impending hostilities. Bill took pictures of most of the ships in the Scheldt and I saw one of them – a fine Hamburg Lloyd – taken into Rosyth as a prize some twelve months later.

We entered Flushing before dark but officialdom had gone home and nobody worried us. We selected our own berth for the night and were not disturbed. Bill and I went ashore for some fresh meat and bread. It was dusk and everything was very still. We walked over the sea locks that connect the Verbreed Canal to the Outer Haven and along the canal side. Only the night before we had been watching a noisy London holiday crowd: now we were walking beside a placid canal with the murmur of voices and the clacking of wooden clogs against the stones. There was music being played somewhere. We went into a shop, a shop of a thousand smells. I picked out the big ones; bacon, coffee beans, paraffin oil, cigars and cheese. On our way back to the boat we stopped to look at some *botters*. A tug rushed by in the outer harbour hooting in Dutch and the ripples chased each other into the darkness. It was time we turned in for we had to be away bright and early the next morning. Little did we think that the Huns would be in Flushing within the twelvemonth and these docks a target for Bomber Command.

The Germans build a pretty ship (this one taken prize in 1940)

"...An Ellerman City Boat"

Chapter Two: Den Helder

Sunday 13th August 1939

We packed up and stowed at 0500, had breakfast and were underway an hour later. There was a bit of a swell at the mouth of the Galgep but the sea calmed down as we got under the lee of the Zouteland Bank. There was very little colour in the morning: only the few green, blue and yellow bathing huts along the sand dunes and the occasional red channel buoy swinging in the tide. Everything else was a shade of grey, forlorn and inexpressibly lovely. The dunes on this south west coast of Walcheren are about fifty feet high and unbroken. We passed Westkappelle close inshore with its lighthouse, three windmills and a cluster of red-roofed houses looking delightfully Dutchesque.

At about twenty to eight the sun broke through and the breeze came up with a moderate sea. Twenty minutes later we passed the Oost Gat Buoy which was groaning and snoring in a most unhappy manner. The breeze steadily freshened and by lunchtime spray was slashing over the foredeck. The wind was just free on the port bow so, after a quick lunch of very solid pork pies, we ran up the mainsail. I don't think it did much good but it probably steadied the boat a bit.

We lunged our way up the Dutch coast all day, making seven and a half to eight knots. It turned into a grand day, blue sky and great white clouds. Off Ijmuiden we passed close to a Dutch fisherman bound for harbour. He waved cheerfully, probably because he would soon be at home with his wife, but we couldn't help feeling "What nice chaps the Dutch are!"

The entrance to the Texel made a pleasant picture. We approached through the Schulpegat at about eight in the evening.

The westing sun lit up huge cumulus clouds hanging low over the land and turned the world softly pink. The tall red lighthouse stood out well and is an excellent seamark.

As we entered Den Helder the Texel Island ferry rather shook us by coming backwards out of the harbour at high speed. Once we had avoided this menace we stationed Fattie aft with instructions to dip to warships. Bill had impressed upon us that Den Helder was the "Dutch Portsmouth...very important place" etc. I don't know what we had expected to see but I rather think that we were disappointed in the small harbour. We didn't realise that most of the smaller naval craft went into a tideless basin and that the great part of the Dutch Navy formed the East Indies Squadron with a smaller force stationed at Curaçoa in the Netherlands West Indies.

We dipped to the cruiser "SUMATRA" but received no reply as she was undergoing a refit. A naval tug waved a greeting so we saluted him. As we passed an old type torpedo boat (probably one of those that would do such good work shelling the Schevingen beach when the Netherlands were overrun in May 1940) Fattie nearly dropped the ensign into the propellers. A very stolid Dutchman ambled aft and returned our salute.

The harbour master had been watching all this time and, interpreting his gesticulations wrongly, we secured alongside some *schakkers*. He came on board and moved us down alongside the lifeboat. The poor old chap seemed very worried about our blue ensign which the Skipper was flying as a member of the Royal Thames Yacht club.

"Are there any British Naval Officers on board?"

"No there are no British Naval Officers on board."

"Then why are you flying zee blue ensign?"

We managed to reassure him and after he had looked at our passports and enjoyed a nip of whisky he was satisfied. The crowd that had gathered to see the English yacht began to disperse except for one or two who could speak English well and came on board for a drink. One of them had served in British merchant ships and became our interpreter. He promised to bring some fresh fish in the morning.

That night we went to a beer house. Here we made the unfortunate acquaintance of the Man With The Stinking Breath. Skips started the trouble by giving him a beer. He was already very drunk and leaned over us exhaling poisonous fumes. Mike and Bill soon moved but Skips and I were trapped. How long we suffered I cannot say until suddenly up jumped Skipper and said we had better be getting back. We came to the unanimous conclusion that the M.W.T.S.B. had swallowed something that had died.

Monday 14ᵗʰ August 1939
NEXT MORNING our interpreter arrived early with a net bag of dabs. It cost us a guilder. I set to and cleaned them and we had a

fine breakfast in a short time. Later the Shell oil lighter came alongside and we took on 500 litres of diesel. Our Dutch friend called for us at 1130 and we went into the town. I was interested to see all the men wearing their dark clothes and round clerical hats. I was able to buy a good pair of clogs and we loaded ourselves up with stores, especially oranges for Germany because it was said that it was not possible to buy them there.

Honest George gutting fish

I had hoped to meet my

brother Jack who was cruising in Dutch waters in a friend's yacht "ATALANTA". I found, after enquiries, that he had left Den Helder two days before. We went back on board and had lunch. That morning I had seen my first submarine coming down the harbour. It was one of the Dutch "O" class. Later, once we were at war, I met a Royal Netherlands Naval officer who had been on the bridge of that same submarine and who remembered "NAROMIS" alongside the lifeboat. Just before we left we were treated by the sight of HNMS "VAN TROMP" coming up the harbour. We waited until she had berthed before we left. She and her sister "JACOB VAN HEEMSKERKE" were originally intended to be large destroyer leaders but finished up as light cruisers. The "HEEMSKERKE" was completed in England and did excellent work in home waters as an anti-aircraft cruiser.

Den Helder: Cruiser "TROMP" in background, Holland

Chapter Three: In German Waters

Monday 14th August 1939

THERE WAS a minor flurry of excitement as we left Willemssoord Den Helder that afternoon. We very nearly ran on to the Hoorder Hanks bank in the entrance to the Texel. The Navigator had slipped up somewhat as it was obvious by the broken water that there was not a channel through. When the lead showed less than a fathom we put both engines into reverse and made for the deep water along the Texel Island coast. Terschelling L.V was sighted just before 5 o'clock. "NAROMIS" was slamming into a short sea, sending sheets of water and spray aft. There was not much to do on hops like this except munch biscuits and listen to the news bulletins from London. We tried twice to get D/F bearings with our set but with little success – probably lack of skill on our part.

A stormy sun went down and we felt lonely and strange steaming into the approaching night. I turned in at about 2030

Picturesque canal in Helder, Holland

feeling rather sick and miserable. The deck was leaking over my bunk and the boat was gavotting round in a most lively manner. We passed the Borkum Riff L.V. during the First Watch. They enquired our name and Bill, who was on watch at the time, replied in Morse.

I had rather trying time during the Middle Watch. We were right in the steamer track and a small yacht's lights are pitifully insignificant. On sighting a steamer it was necessary to alter course in good time because, with the tide against us, we were not making more than five and a half knots over the ground. To make matters worse I was feeling vaguely sick without the relief of sickness. It was a fine night and I found it easier to steer by a bright star instead of always peering into the binnacle.

Tuesday 15th August 1939

THAT MIDDLE and Morning Watch were the longest I ever remember keeping. Towards the end I got sleepy and wholly un-nautical for in the half light of dawn I steered by the nose of a cloud man. Two of us were on together, which was a good arrangement as it prevented the helmsman from going to sleep. Bill was relieved by Mike at 0400 and I by Fattie at 0800. By 0555 we had reached the Norderney L.V. which was scarlet in the early morning sun. Course was altered to 102° for the Weser.

Later, when I awoke, we were nearing the Elbe IV L.V. and all hands turned out to make our vessel shipshape before entering Cuxhaven. Decks were sluiced down, the mainsail stowed (we had had a following wind from Norderney) and the medical and Dutch flags hoisted at the yard. Also, before we were in sight of the German coast, we changed our blue ensign for the red, remembering our experience at Den Helder.

Our entrance to Cuxhaven was bad. There was quite a crowd at the west entrance pier to watch us berth and of course we

Fish Harbour, Cuxhaven, Germany

made a hash of it. We turned round, proceeded to sea again and tried a second time making a rather undignified dart into the Fischerhafen. Customs, police and two or three others Heil Hitlered their way into the aft cabin. Reserve was broken down with some Scotch and after a lot of particulars had been taken on a lot of printed forms and a few more Heils, the examination was over. They took a list of all the food, spirits and tobacco on board, a large portion of which had to be sealed in a sack for the passage through the Kiel Canal.

We were all anxious to go ashore and have a look at these people who had so disturbed our world for the last three years. We lunched at the Dölles Hotel quite well. My first impressions were ugly, cheap-looking motor cars and comely flaxen-haired girls with delicious blue eyes. That afternoon Mike went to the bathing pool and I suspected it was to keep the latter under observation. The rest of us went back to the boat to sleep off the München Biere.

That evening we asked the crew of the Hamburg yacht "CONDOR II" on board and for the second time that day Scotch was a good ambassador. We parted friends, promising to meet later in the evening. Three of us took a snatch of supper and proceeded ashore to the largest dance hall. The dancers were all very stiff and North German, nobody seemed to be really enjoying themselves. The evening progressed and we joined our three Hamburgian friends, Henry, Foss and Kurt over some cognac. We made, I remember, a horrible mixture of the drinks: whisky, Moselle, cognac, kirsch, beer and schnapps. As the evening wore on I developed a very pronounced French accent, much to my horror. Presently we got a taxi and doodled off to a little hell where the drinks were twice as expensive. Everyone became very friendly and all Anglo-German difficulties were overcome. The French and Italians were consigned to the depths and many other temporary political adjustments made.

Poor old Foss began to make violent love to Fattie so I was forced to pour my beer all over him, whereupon he fell flat on the floor. It was time we made for the dock so, bursting into song we passed down the main street of Cuxhaven singing "Land of Hope and Glory", the "Horst Wessel" etc. On arriving back at the dock Kurt promptly fell in. This sobered him up a bit and he managed to get into "CONDOR II"'s dinghy. Mike fell into our dinghy and dragged himself aboard. Fattie was saying a last farewell to Herr Foss when I started to ferry myself to the stern of "NAROMIS" which was lying about ten yards off the pontoon. Fattie, suffering from the illusion that the dinghy was still alongside, stepped into the water with a yell and a colossal splash. My humane efforts to save the poor chap were disregarded and the *bon-vivant* tried to pull me in as well, just to make a party of it.

Chapter Four: The Kiel Canal

Wednesday 16th August 1939

NEXT MORNING Mike and I went ashore to try and get a chicken. It was rather jolly trying to make ourselves understood and the shop-people were as helpful as they could be. Food seemed fairly plentiful and, generally speaking, cheaper than in England. Our precautions in getting oranges in Holland were unnecessary as they abounded here at forty pfennigs a half kilo. Our chicken hunt, however, was not a success. All that Cuxhaven could produce that morning was a stunted little *huhn* which was commanding an uneconomic price. Instead we bought some sausage and hurried back for breakfast.

Our friends from "CONDOR II" came out to watch us leave the harbour looking, I thought, rather sheepish. Poor fellows, they probably had an oriental hangover. We got away without mishap and set our course for Brunsbüttel. The port motor caused some anxious moments because the oil pressure had dropped for no apparent reason. Skips got very filthy taking down the oil filter whilst we proceeded at reduced speed. We were dribbling up the Elbe when a German tramp steamer made a determined assault on us. She overtook us fine on the starboard quarter and would have sliced us in two with utter disregard had not someone chanced to come out of the wheel house at that moment. Helm hard a-port and full astern port engine saved us but it was close, damn close.

Soon after this incident we picked up the pilot; a little rotund fellow with very little to say and proceeded into the first lock of the Noord-Ostsee Kanal. Together there were four other ships waiting in the lock: two of them were Swedish and two were German. As there was some time to spare, some of us got onto the cattermorans that keep ships away from the lock side and then up onto the lock side

We wandered over to look at the old outer harbour on the Brunsbüttelkoog side and were intrigued to find four U-Boats alongside each other. They were of the 740 type and had obviously come from the canal to go out on patrol. I was struck by the youthfulness of the officers on the bridges of the U-boats. Although these may only have been Third Hands or *Leutnants zur See* they seemed to be about nineteen and looked utterly humourless. A whistle blew. The ratings cast off the breast wires and the first submarine headed out into the Elbe under her main engines. When she was a half cable away, the crew of the second sprang to attention and did likewise with absolute precision; then the third and then the fourth. I believe that it was one of these U-boats that would be responsible for torpedoing the "ATHENIA" within four hours of war being declared, less than three weeks later – thus opening unrestricted submarine warfare where it had been left off in 1918.

Suddenly another whistle blew (everything seemed to work by whistles) and we hurried on board "NAROMIS". The lock gate was sliding into the wall. An engine-room telegraph rang and the steamer ahead of us, the Swedish "KIRUNA", moved slowly into the Kaiser Wilhelm Canal. We followed closely and soon were in the ninety kilometre stretch that connects the North Sea to the Baltic.

The first few miles is embanked and by standing on our cabin roof we could look down onto flat meadows, very like East Anglia. The early afternoon was misty with heat and lent soft colour to the grazing cows and horses and to the little farms. The pasture faded away into the horizon of Holstein and the world was very peaceful. Children on the embankment waved to us as we passed – waved and smiled at the hated English.

There was great variety in the ships passing up and down the canal: a Dutchman with Scandinavian wood, then a Greek with pit-props, a little green schooner, the "ZEEHUND", followed by a great wall-sided tramp from Panama in ballast. There were several *scoops* sailing down the waterway, often with a heavy list and their sterns cocked in the air. Some vessels wore a canvas cylinder at their masthead, indicating that they were to be given the deep water channel as they were deep laden.

A few kilometres from Brunsbüttel we came upon dredgers widening and deepening the canal. It was intended that it should be able to take 35,000 ton ships by 1940, the battleships of the "BISMARK" class in particular. Evidence at the time of writing suggests that this work was not completed before these ships were commissioned and that they have never passed through the canal, always going north through the Great Belt and the Kattegat.

Further on the scenery changed and the low-lying country gave place to high cliffs on either side of the canal. These were for the most part well-wooded and smelled sweetly of warm bracken. Some of the bridges we passed under were impressive and we were sorry we could not take photos of them. The pilot we had for the first part of the canal was a nice old chap who spoke English well and seemed to like us. About half way we changed pilots for a somewhat younger man who was surly and arrogant. At six o'clock we had eased down to listen to the news from London. We could only just get it, being so far away and it was the last we heard for some time.

There we were, ghosting down the Kiel Canal, listening to the grave tidings. There had been a skirmish on the Polish frontier, a guard had been killed, ration cards were ready and war seemed inevitable. The German pilot was staring ahead of him, slightly apart from us, also listening and understanding that war was very close. Suddenly he shouted, "Full speed, hard a-starboard!" Ahead of us, round the bend of the canal came two of Germany's latest destroyers, "KARL GALSTER" and "ERIC GIESE". Bill went aft and dipped to them. The Germans saluted and some of the sailors waved to us in a friendly manner. This was typical of the way in which we were received all through Germany. Some people were naturally more strained but nowhere did we find anything but good will. Politics was not, however, discussed to any great degree.

It took us seven hours to pass from the western locks to Holtenau at the Baltic end, through fields of harvested rye and wheat, past be-smocked and straw-hatted *fraus* helping their menfolk with the harvest, and past parties of children who waved and smiled. We were not kept waiting long for the great lock gates to open and let the tiny "NAROMIS" in. The lock that would take a battleship worked for us alone that evening.

It was dusk when we proceeded out into the Kieler Fjord and turned our bows towards the Olympia-Hafen. Going up the fjord we passed the 8" heavy cruiser "ADMIRAL HIPPER" about three cables away. I was rather amused when, on returning to England I read an article in the *Times* discussing the strength of the German fleet: "It is not known whether the German cruiser 'ADMIRAL HIPPER' is in commission yet." Next morning she was gone so I was glad we had seen her in the twilight.

On our arrival at Olympia-Hafen an official came down from the Yacht Club of Germany and invited us to use the club during our stay, a kind offer we took advantage of. We were berthed snugly in the corner of the *hafen* and, after thoroughly gilding their respective lilies, the crew of "NAROMIS" stepped ashore with business in their eyes and Reich marks in their pockets and made a beeline for the Yacht Club. Here we had the most noble and capacious dish I can remember. It was called the "Yacht Club Platte" and was far more than we could eat. I for one wished we could have taken it back on board and finished it for breakfast. It consisted principally of anchovies and smoked salmon on rye bread and butter, veal, *petit pois*, French beans, German asparagus, fried eggs, tomatoes, lettuce, cucumbers and lots of other things which I cannot now call to mind. This was washed down with beer and also Hollands gin with orange juice.

When we were replete we took stock of our surroundings through the smoke of "stinkadores". We had dined in the ballroom of the Club. Two great paintings dominated the room: Hindenburg and Hitler. The Kaiser must have danced often in this room, while his yacht "METEOR" was in the fjord. There were quite a number of naval officers using the club and as they passed us, with their ceremonial dirks swinging at their sides, they greeted us with "Heil Hitler". It was the greeting we used ourselves after a bit, getting accustomed to it.

Thursday 17th August 1939
THURSDAY WAS born a beautiful day and after breakfast we went shopping in Kiel. My first tram ride in Germany was a free one. There are two compartments, one where you stand with the driver and the other where you pay extra and have a seat. I sat while Bill and Mike rode with the driver but no one asked me for the fare so I concluded Bill had paid for me. This slight advantage was counteracted by the unfortunately strong garlic breath of my neighbour which nearly vanquished me before the ride was over. Our impressions of Kiel were good. The roads were leafy and the whole town seemed clean and pleasant.

We all got off at the Innerhafen and I bought something I had coveted for years – a German pipe with a lid. Bill and I walked along the dockside and looked at some of Germany's new constructions in various stages of completion. When we arrived back at "NAROMIS" for lunch we discovered that the battlecruiser "GNEISENAU" and the cruisers "LIEPZIG", "NURNBERG" and a "K" class had come in. While we were eating the "KOLN" came up the fjord, turned in a surprisingly small circle and brought up at a buoy. Away went the whaler's crew and she was shackled up efficiently. I could see about two score ratings exercising on the quarter deck in bathing slips. They looked fit and very sunburnt. Another point of interest was that the main armament was <u>aft</u> with the turrets staggered: "X" on the port side and "Y" to starboard. This was an experiment, I understand, so that these guns could be brought on a more forrard bearing <u>in case she was chasing</u> in a fight and not retiring.

The afternoon was spent pleasantly. Fattie was in the engine room changing the "schmeeroyle". He was an imperial sight in his long flannel shorts hanging well below his knees and his well-nourished body schmeered with oyle. The others of the crew tried to get some of the weed scraped off the boot-topping and spent the afternoon bathing. There was a bit of a flurry in the evening when our agent hurried on board to tell us that we couldn't get any diesel in Germany. This was a shock as we had intended locking back into the canal, oiling and then pressing on to Warnemunde where we would meet Mr Clutton's daughter, Iris, who was staying in Berlin. We had made arrangements to oil at six o'clock the next morning but now these special orders seemed so significant that we thought it was time to start moving.

A hurried conference was called after we had got rid of the agent. The facts were these. We had eight hours steaming left in both tanks. If diesel was not obtainable in Germany our only alternative was to make for the nearest Danish port which a hurried glance at the chart showed us to be Nakskov on the island of Laaland. We would sail on the morrow for Denmark.

We commenced our last night in Germany by going to a rather indifferent cabaret. Bill, Mike and I left the other two, slightly pickled, talking earnestly to the barmaid and did a beer hall crawl. I have dim recollections of dancing with a fish-eyed maiden, drinking lots of Holstein beer with Steinhäger schnapps as a chaser.

Kiel, Innerhafen. Germany

Chapter Five: The Danish Islands

Friday August 18th 1939

NEXT MORNING I went up into the town to buy some milk and get a loaf. I was treated to the sight of the Kiel citizens lining up for their gas masks at what seemed to me an extraordinary hour, seven o'clock in the morning. Things must be pretty serious for them to be issued at all. My mind rushed back to the September crisis of a year before. I got the milk and bread and hurried back to the ship. Less than an hour later we were steaming down the fjord at an economical speed bound for Nakskov.

Accompanying us seawards were a couple of minesweepers and a mine layer with a load of black sinister-looking mines. Possibly she was on her way to block the Little Belt channel. There were also two small 250-ton U-boats of the type called "North Sea Ducks." These are used for coastal patrol duties and for training. There was no apparent escort for these two submarines who were carrying out independent diving exercises. This seemed to me to be a somewhat hazardous operation in such a crowded area but I supposed the Germans knew what they were doing. A torpedo boat raced past us at twenty knots as we were approaching Laboe to clear customs. It caused havoc in the galley. As we had got away in such a hurry the duty galley slaves had not started to wash up. Piles of dishes crashed onto the deck, followed by a thermos flask that went off like a small bomb.

By 0930 we were mooring alongside the jetty at Laboe. It was a pleasant little place and I was sorry when we left, only half an hour later. On our starboard beam was the great German naval war memorial to all those who had died in the 1914 war. It was shaped as a rudder and stood out against the sky at the head of the Kieler Fjord. One of the navy's sail training ships was distant on our port bow. It was either the "HORST WESSEL" or the "LEO SCHLAGETER" but we were too far away to be sure which.

Once we were out at sea the log had been showing a steady six knots on the three-quarter throttle and everything was well when suddenly a vessel on our starboard side opened fire with a 3.5" across our bows. We were a bit perturbed at first then we realised it was not intended for us but for a target bearing red 70° estimated range 7000 yards. On our present course we were steaming on into the middle of a private battle so we altered course and passed under the stern of the vessel which had fired. We caught up with her at the end of her first run and passed her about fifty yards way, gently lifting to the slight swell that was coming from the Fehmarn Belt. It was the gunnery school tender "FUCHS". At the time I thought that the shooting was indifferent but I realise now that the bricks were pitching very fairly.

At 1230 we sighted Kielsnof lighthouse standing out well in the noonday sun. This was our first glimpse of Denmark and we all felt pleased with ourselves and vaguely relieved. The atmosphere in Germany had been tense and now we could kick up our heels and behave in a fairly normal manner. For the last half hour of our trip we had been escorted by one of Germany's new "M" class minesweepers. She may have had instructions to see us on our way because she turned back when we reached Danish territorial waters.

Skipper told us that the Reich marks we have will be worth more in Danish kroner. That was pleasant. The Danish coast was pleasant; the sun was warm and the Baltic was blue – so it was a well-contented ship's company that settled to lunch that Friday.

The Langeland coast was fascinating in a modest way. There were no great hills or long stretches of flat but country at its best – white farmhouses, generally thatched, surrounded by slopes of stubble and meadow. The houses all had very white walls and chimneys together with scarlet roofs which contrasted with the

Nakskov, Denmark

clumps of trees looking cool and green on the rising ground. The only peculiarity was the six-armed windmills dotted around. These seemed to be a local feature because we did not see them anywhere else in Denmark. This landscape is inextricably influenced by the sea. Sheep graze down to the water's edge; the labourer can leave his plough and set his nets on posts placed along the shore. The Baltic here is practically tideless and sufficiently sheltered for a thatched boat house to have been built right to the water's edge.

WE LOGGED eight miles up the coast of Langeland then turned four points to starboard so as to arrive at the entrance to Nakskov fjord. I am sure that we did not take the right channel in. It was not clear on our rather small scale chart and, if I remember rightly, *The Baltic Pilot* didn't help much either. We found ourselves in very shoal water but somehow escaped going aground and eventually passed into the northern channel by the island of Enehøje. After that it was plain steaming along a well-buoyed channel to Nakskov.

I think I enjoyed this visit to Laaland and the subsequent trip to Copenhagen more than any other two days in the whole voyage. This was neutral time. We were not now urged to get on as quickly as possible; neither were we obsessed by the threat of War. We had left that behind in Germany and were not to pick it up again until the next week. Nakskov was not disposed to talk about it and we were grateful. It seemed to belong to a peaceful world untainted by greed or lust for power or hatred or discontent.

The fjord charmed me. It has a tricky entrance but anyone cruising these waters should not hesitate to give the little town a visit. Once past Enehøje it broadens out into a great expanse of shallow water and gives a marvellous impression of space. There is a deep, well-marked channel and one passes tiny islands or holms which are for the most part uninhabited save for an occasional bathing party with a couple of sailing boats pulled up on the beach. Everyone we met waved and grinned a welcome and, when we eventually arrived at the quay, swarms of fair-haired children arrived from nowhere and practically pushed each other into the water in their agitation to see the yacht. Very few English yachts visit Nakskov as it is rather in a backwater and we should have missed it had it not been for the fuel embargo at Kiel.

We had to move "NAROMIS" as the ferry from Germany was due. When we had done this, two green-clothed Customs officials came on board. At first they were for sealing up all our booze but after a glass or two of schnapps they became very reasonable. The Chief of Police arrived too and proceeded to make himself very much at home, airing his English and his cigars until the cabin became unbearable. The English language is a free currency in Denmark. Children learn it in all the schools so we had little difficulty making ourselves understood. Cigars are also used a lot in preference to cigarettes. For instance when I went along to order the fuel my wants were attended to in perfect English and I was pressed to a cigar. It seemed my trip along the quay, smoking my lidded pipe and clad in sailing sweater, piratical scarf and clogs caused quite a stir amongst the inhabitants!

That evening we changed into our shore-side clothes and went to look around the town. Whether it was because Nakskov was my first Danish town, it appealed to me immensely. It seemed prosperous and at the same time determined that progress should not disturb its well-ordered life. A considerable shipyard, owned I believe by the East Asiatic company, is placed well away from the old town on the opposite side of the fjord. After we had wandered around the old streets we returned to the main square and sat in the open air at a café drinking Pilsner and watching 1924 model Fords rattling round. After some food and a dance or two at the main dance hall, the "Bristol", we went back to the boat and turned in comparatively sober.

A street in Nakskov, Denmark

Saturday August 19ᵗʰ 1939

SATURDAY WAS another brilliant day and everyone was up early. The diesel arrived in a lorry and the business of fuelling started. I stole this opportunity of taking myself off to visit the church and I think I can honestly say that of all the churches I have been in this one was the most exactly perfect. I have been unable to find any literature on the subject but I should say that it was late fifteenth century, built of small bricks with the familiar crow-stepped tower surmounted with a fine spire. The interior was lofty and the walls white-washed and spotless. No dim religious light here and the simplicity of the architecture showed the ornate sixteenth century altar and pulpit to perfection. The carved organ loft would have done credit to Grinling Gibbons himself. I saw something in this church that I have never seen before – namely a model sailing ship about forty inches long, suspended from the roof and placed so that the candles would light up its sails. Denmark depends so much on the sea that this old vessel seemed more than appropriate in this lovely church.

The process of oiling had not quite finished when I returned so Mike and I swung out the dinghy and rowed down the harbour with our bathing gear. It was a perfect day for a swim and we floundered about for half an hour. I was particularly interested in the small fishing boats of about 24'. They were clinker built and the most graceful lines, beamy with a canoe stern. I had foolish dreams about buying one here or having one built, say, next year? Next year never comes but I can't say I have forgotten that idea – "after the war..."

We got underway after we had said goodbye to the Chief of Police and other friendly folk and we proceeded down the fjord. Our plan was to have some more bathing and then lunch before pressing on to Copenhagen via the Storstrøm. We anchored – or rather we threw the anchor overboard and remained in its immediate vicinity, lying

Bathing off the Swedish coast   *Shocking!*

Jock and Mike

in two fathoms off a tiny holm with a sandy beach. It was grand fun running the length of the foredeck then diving naked into the clear water, then sitting out in the sun and eating smoked salmon and German black bread with 'butter' made from, amongst other things, whale oil. When the others went to dinner I stayed for a moment on deck to listen to the stillness. The only sound was a faint lipping of the water on the nearby islet and an occasional seabird. Soon we should be underway again, the two engines drowning out all these things, so, while it lasted it was refreshing and I still have the picture of this great stretch of sunlit water fixed in my memory.

It was just before three o'clock when "NAROMIS" left the fjord and turned north along the coast of Laaland. There had been some discussion about whether we should go southabout by way of the Fehmarn Belt and Cadet Canal and then up the eastern coast of Falster to Copenhagen, or take the narrow northern channel. We decided that the latter would be more interesting and "NAROMIS", built as she was on the Broads, drew remarkably little water. So, north we turned and by quarter to six we were passing Rågo which

Trading ketch in Storstrøm, Denmark

is really the entrance to the Storstrøm. It was an island of about fifty acres as far as I could judge with a farm and four or five white washed cottages, half a dozen meadows and fields and a small pier. This was indeed a place to return to and possess as soon as possible. For a thousand or so kroner the Lord of Rågo could build a fishing yacht and live the rest of his days as completely self-supporting and independent as it is possible to do in this world.

By the time we reached Orehoved, a tiny port at the southern end of the Storstrøm bridge, it was getting dark. Orehoved used to be the ferry port between Sjaelland and Falster but has not been used for some years now. After we had secured ourselves to the jetty we went ashore to stretch our legs and to see anything that there was to see in the starlight. As we walked up the little lane from the dock I remember thinking how like England it was; the smell of the hedgerows, the chatter of the crickets, even the tarred road seemed familiar. Presently the village store showed its friendly lights and we made our way across to see if they had any potatoes or fruit.

The shopkeeper was a retired sailor called Earling Anderson. We spoke at first in German but he did not seem disposed to serve us at this late hour. When he learned we were English however his whole manner changed. He had served on British ships and spoke the language well: it was not possible for him to do enough to help us. Certainly we could have potatoes; his brother-in-law would go into the garden and dig some up for us. This, remember, was at night when most of the family had already retired. The charming fellow insisted on making us coffee and sandwiches; his wife was called and introduced, even the baby was dragged out of bed to be admired. Then the neighbours were roused and by the time we were ready to return to the yacht quite an assembly had gathered, all offering to carry something back for us.

We experienced similar friendly feelings everywhere we went in Denmark. Great Britain's stock was very high whereas the feeling towards Germany was mainly one of fear though public attitudes were strictly correct. For Denmark, as a small, practically unarmed state, whose export trade was almost entirely divided between Great Britain and Germany, it was not possible to be anything other than neutral when facing the forthcoming conflict. Earling Anderson said, "Here in Denmark we eat, drink and are very glad." His shop was a fine example of that statement: it stocked everything from tinned tunny to corsets!

Naromis *at Orehoved. Bill on deck. Denmark*

Chapter Six: Copenhagen

Sunday August 20th 1939

WE WERE under way by 0840 the next morning and were blessed with another fine day. Bill managed to take some excellent photographs of the bridge. It is the longest in Europe and was built by Dorman Long of Middlesbrough. Nothing of special interest occurred on the trip through the islands to the Bogø Strom. The scenery was pleasant with cornfields rising from the water's edge or heavily wooded islets with a cluster of white, thatched houses or perhaps a quay with a pink-washed barn standing back among the trees. The channels are too shallow to be used by anything other than yachts or the Baltic trading ketches and these backwaters would make an ideal cruising ground for a summer holiday. Yachtsmen might object that it is too far from home waters to get there in the limited time at their disposal but the answer is to hire a local boat. There is wonderful scope – the Little Belt, the beautiful Funean waters and Sweden within reach. For anyone "going foreign" this part of the Baltic is worth considering for its attractive scenery, its mainly sheltered and almost tideless waters and, above all, for its kindly, helpful people.

The Bogø Strom whistle buoy was astern at noon. Through the Storstrøm we had been able to see the bottom up to three fathoms but now the water became deeper and the seas shorter until we were pitching in quite an excited manner. I went for an afternoon zizz and was awakened by Bill enquiring whether I would like to see a four-masted schooner and a barque under sail. I was out of my bunk at the double and on deck in far less time than it takes to type this. The sun was setting behind Copenhagen making a fascinating silhouette of the city with its domes and spires sharp

Naromis *in Copenhagen*

Yachts of all nations: Swedish, Polish, British, German, Danish

against the summer sky. At least two hundred yachts large and small were scattered over the blue sea with their white sails gleaming. It was a fine sight.

We proceeded up the harbour to the yacht basin and moored head to quay with a rope astern to a buoy. Skips asked the yacht master about Customs. He shrugged his shoulders and smiled: "They may come tonight or tomorrow morning. If they come, they come..." He gave the impression that such things should be ignored.

I don't intend to say much about the capital of Denmark. It is – or at least it was, before the German occupation – a most delightful city. The people are as friendly as the rest of the country and it has an air of gaiety and make-believe. There is the renowned Tivoli, a gigantic fair but not in the English way. It costs about sixpence to go in and everybody goes. There are open air displays of acrobatics, pantomimes, plays as well as ghost tunnels and fat women. Everything is orderly and there is not the incessant din of the year-before-last's hottest number blaring from a steam organ. There are jazz and military bands as well as a fine orchestra. When we were there the trees were hung with Chinese lanterns and bunches of coloured electric bulbs like grapes on a vine. The waterfalls were floodlit and an old frigate was moored in one of the lakes, its masts and spars outlined with little electric lights. Up the gangway and we could drink our *stein* of Coburg Pilsner and listen to an accordion band. High above all of this was the floodlit tower of the town hall, coppered and standing out blue-green against the indigo sky.

Monday August 21ˢᵗ 1939
MONDAY CAME and went in a flash. We spent it collecting mail, gawping at historic buildings and sunbathing. In the evening we all went to the aerodrome to meet the skipper's daughter. She had been staying with a high official of the Nazi party in Berlin and the

A very delightful Danish girl

Some fine buildings, Malmö

situation looked so grave that it was decided we should take her out of Germany with us.

Tuesday August 22nd 1939
THE NEXT day was fine so we took "NAROMIS" across the Sound to the Swedish coast and anchored in Sallviken Bay some miles north of Malmö. The Sound was choppy and the short steep seas cascaded spray over us but we managed to find a lee, close inshore and had lunch on the foc's'le. Then we got the companion way out and had some bathing after which we up-anchored and made for Malmö. The town itself was comparatively uninteresting but it was my first Swedish soil.

We were sitting in a café drinking Klass II beer when we picked up a newspaper and discovered that Germany had made a pact with Russia. I couldn't understand much of the Swedish but the price of War Loan 88 1/2 was eloquent enough. The ship's company wasn't very gay when we left Malmö that evening, returning to Copenhagen. We had to decide what to do should War break out. The original plan included passing though the Limn fjord from the Baltic back into the North Sea at Esjberg, thence south to the Frisian Islands, Ostend and back to Ramsgate. It was clear this route would be too dangerous and an alternative would have to be conceived if the worst came to the worst. We could not go back through the Kiel Canal so the only possibility was north to Norway and a long leg over to the Scottish coast.

Wednesday August 23rd 1939
WEDNESDAY DAWNED fair and cloudless. We spent the morning going over the Tuxborg Brewery, one of the most important beer foundries in the world. The tour was concluded by sampling about a dozen kinds of brew, including Imperial Ale-Porter (double strength). This fortified us to go to the British Legation to hear

the latest news. I remember how cool and pleasant it seemed in the Legation after the noon heat and the stifling atmosphere of rumour and fact. The Russians, it appeared, had concluded a non-aggression pact with Germany. The German army would be fully mobilised by tonight and, according to the *Times* correspondent who had arrived from Berlin that morning, the frontiers would be closed within a few hours. Nothing more could be said and all we could do was to report our presence to the consulate and wire the Skipper's niece to take the first airliner from Berlin. We would set out for home as soon as she arrived.

A very delightful Danish girl came on board in the afternoon then, about three o'clock, we got underway and motored up the Sound to Bellevue, the resort north of Copenhagen. Here we bathed and had tea and became acquainted with the "Canoeing Count". He was a young Swedish gentleman, aged about 21, who came paddling out to us in his canoe. He spoke English well and introduced himself as Ulph, Count of H___? It was a sunny afternoon and he and I talked for a bit before I took him below for tea. The conversation turned to war and he predicted that it would start by Germany attacking Poland and after a little while Russia would march in from the East and the Nazis and the Soviets would divide up the Polish Republic between them. In less than a month his words were an accomplished fact.

Ulph, Mike and I went out to supper and we had a very entertaining evening – our last in charming Copenhagen – dancing at the arena until the early hours. When we returned to Langelinie where the "NAROMIS" was berthed we found a Polish yacht on one side of her and a big German motor yacht on the other. We had visions of implementing the Government's guarantee to Poland if the German made an attack but he was off the next morning, recalled to the Fatherland. He was the last peaceful German we spoke to. He said how sorry he was that the situation looked so bad and he trusted things would soon be alright.

The War bogey was hard on our heels again and from now the cruise took on a more serious aspect. It was apparent that we needed to get away from this land-locked Baltic at our best speed. While we waited for the Skipper's niece to join us, Mike and I made the acquaintance of our future Allies, the Poles.

Chapter Seven:
Elsinore and Kronberg Castle

Thursday August 24th 1939

NEXT MORNING Mike and I went surf-riding in a Swedish motor-cruiser "HOTTAN" with the Poles. Its owner, Peter, had been cruising the Baltic single-handed and had arrived a couple of days ago from Bornholm. He was full of praise for the beauty of the rocky island off the southern tip of Sweden and we wished we could have called there. But there was no dallying now. Skipper's niece would be joining us at any moment and except for a few last minute arrangements we were ready for our trip northwards.

The surf-riding was the greatest fun. It was a warm hazy day with little waves dancing to the *cappriccio* of a summer breeze. Peter would stop the "HOTTAN" and someone would dive onto the limpid water and swim out to the surf-board, lie on it and, when everything was set, off would go the motor-cruiser at twelve or fourteen knots. Then the rider climbed up onto the board, grasped the reins and the fun started. The party went magnificently despite the fact that no one could speak Polish. With the help of some red wine that Peter produced, everyone was talking *haut voix* in a horrible mixture of signs, broken German, French, Swedish and English!

Just before we sailed I had word that our agents, Georg Sorenson, had a package for me which I had been expecting since we arrived in Copenhagen, so I rushed up into the town to collect it and if possible, a *Times* from the Hotel Angleterre (present headquarters of the German army of occupation). The *Times* had not arrived by noon as usual so I decided to walk back along the Bredgade. Here I met one of the counsellors or secretaries to the

Some fine wrought iron work.
Looking towards St Nicholas Church, Copenhagen

Hamlet's castle, Elsinore, Denmark

legation and exchanged a few last words with him. Chamberlain's letter to Hitler had been rejected and war was inevitable. The only slim hope of a settlement of the crisis lay with Mussolini. My friend seemed relieved by this explanation of the worst—and indeed it seemed the only answer.

As soon as I returned "NAROMIS" slipped and proceeded to the Royal Yacht Club to take in a supply of drinking water. On our way out of the harbour, we said goodbye to the little mermaid who lives on a rock in the harbour, near Langelinie. This statue is something to fall in love with, the most charming thing in charming Copenhagen. It is curious now in going through life we come across something that is perfectly fashioned to our particular taste: a church, a piece of wrought-iron, a snatch of a Bach cantata, a poem, a piece of Venetian glass, a yacht – something so occasional and fine that it stands out sharply against a background of praiseworthy things. The little mermaid is one of those things.

It was foggy in the Sound. The summer haze of the morning had developed into something more potent, but although it cut the visibility down, the S.E. breeze did not allow it to impede our progress towards Elsinore. We arrived just after six and secured to the town quay. Another yacht arrived soon after we did and, being much larger, rather stole our thunder. The crowd of wise men and boys that come and gape over the quay on such occasions moved in a flock to look at "WHITE EAGLE", a steam yacht built in Southampton in the 1880s. They must have felt a little hurt when the old ship cast off and moved over to the privacy of the opposite side of the harbour. We noticed she was flying the red ensign.

Danish ports seem to combine and blend industry with antiquity quite successfully. We arrived in time to hear the last bustle in the ship-building yard on the other side of the harbour. When the last riveter stopped splitting the air, a veil of silence fell on the town. Two ancients sitting on the quay with rod and line

Elsinore, Denmark

were lifeless. Renaissance houses, built obliquely on the quay, whispered amongst themselves. The age-green church spire presided over the meeting as it had done for the last four hundred years and more. Dim lights appeared in the growing dusk, men and women moved strangely silent over the rough stones.

"Come on, if you're going to see Kronberg tonight!" I scrambled into the dinghy that Mike had got alongside and soon we were humming over the flat water to Hamlet's Castle, the outboard making foul noises. Unfortunately the castle itself was shut but we wandered about the ground, guideless, unattended except by imagination. It had been a warm day and the scent of lime trees hung in the air. There was, too, the sense of the calamity that was threatening the world, making the peace of these old walls almost unbearable. Perhaps it was the ghost talking to himself about things "to be". I walked out onto the ramparts and had a look at the fifteen cannon guarding the Sound. They had been cast by Christian VII to command the Narrows but nowadays this duty is assigned to indicator loops, patrolling aircraft and minefields.

As Mike and I returned across the harbour we saw the "WHITE EAGLE's" boat approaching "NAROMIS". Cursing, as we remembered that the rest of the company had gone to town, we hung on tightly and opened up our 90cc single-lung outboard to close on three knots and crouching low, we just made it before our prospective guests shoved off. It was the ex-Danish Consul in London and his son and, when Skips returned, he found quite a party in progress. The old gentleman, who I gathered was half English, swore that he had been shadowed by Nazi planes all the way up the Sound and was not a little perturbed about it. We had also seen and commented on these continuous patrols. He was of the opinion that now was the time to go and we could only agree with him.

That evening "the crew" entertained "the girls" at the local dance hall while the Skipper and Jock returned the Consul's visit.

Chapter Eight: Under the Night

Friday August 25th 1939
"... the evening sky / And smelt the sea, and heard the waves / And the seagull's mocking cry" (Brooke)

THE CRISIS develops. There are rumours that the Bank Rate is 4%. There is more mobilisation, the calling up of reserves. The Government is asking for emergency powers – and so on. Both Bill and I were in the RNVSR (Royal Naval Volunteer Supplementary Reserve), he as a potential executive officer and I as a paymaster, so we fretted a little and got the ship out of the harbour with unusual alacrity. Actually, I had cause to worry (had I but known) because my call-up papers had already arrived on the 24th – the day before! We couldn't do more than press on at our best speed and put our faith in the quixotic angel that looks after foolish yachtsmen.

It was in that state of supressed excitement that we stopped the engines at 1030 to hear the news from London and President Roosevelt's further appeal to Europe. We were off Kullen Point and a light breeze on the starboard quarter was enough to fill the sails and keep the patent log turning over. Everything seemed oddly quiet after the noise of the two diesel engines when suddenly there came the sound of gunfire on the port beam. Perhaps the war had already started and our light forces were already in the Kattegat! A dozen suggestions – from naval battles to rock blasting – came to overwrought imaginations. Probably it was a Swedish coast defence ship or the like at firing practice but it made a deep impression on us.

During the morning the wind held astern then took itself off, leaving us on an oily swell. The afternoon saw us off the Swedish

George enjoys the sun

Gothenburg, Sweden

Riviera coast making a steady eight-and-a-half to nine knots with a favourable current. When not watch-keeping I sunbathed and read (considering the state of uncertainty) a very unsuitable book about the last war, full of blood-curdling experiences.

Evening found the Kattegat in an amiable mood. We kept about five miles off the Swedish coast but even at this distance the air was laden with the scent of pine trees. The coast here is very indefinite, studded with thousands of bays and tiny islands. The charts apologise for not printing them all but indeed the hydrographers have done very well inserting the thousands that they have.

The uncanny gleam of the navigation lights was quenched by the moon which rose astern of us. Minutes passed like the hiss of bubbles joining our wake which stretched into the dim distance. Time had no meaning: only the pale stars and the tumbling, pitiless waves had meaning. It would be terrible to fall over board tonight into that loneliness of grey water. There would be no chance.

We closed the coast before midnight and picked up the Fladen Flak at the entrance to Gothenburg Fjord. The moon had gone down into the sea and the night was dark by the time we were weaving our way through the dozens of rocky islets in the fjord. The navigation is made simple by sectored lights fixed on some rock or islands. Keep the green ahead for Piccadilly. Sweden's principal port greeted us with a thousand blazing lights as we steamed up the fjord. A Customs launch intercepted us and directed us to the Customs wharf where we stayed for the few remaining hours of the night.

Chapter Nine: Passage to Norway

Saturday August 26ᵗʰ 1939

IN THE morning we moved the boat higher up towards the town to replenish our stores. On the way up the harbour I saw a sight I don't expect to see again: four of the world's barques alongside each other. I wonder where they are now, back in their home in the Åland Islands perhaps or carrying Finnish timber to Germany in the summer months. No more sailings from Spencer or St Vincent Gulfs until after the war and then perhaps they will come back into their own for a time – if there are the seamen left to man them.

Everyone we met was most kind and very eager for the downfall of Hitler – they rather treated us as instruments to that downfall. Stevedores stopped their work and waved their caps as we went by; a glass or two in the local became a glass or six at the insistence of budding Anglo-maniacs.

We got away at noon after we had fuelled and the water boat had paid us a visit. The Log was streamed in the Vinga Fjord and a course set to take us south of Marstrand to the Skagen-Rev Blink L.V. It was in this area that Lt. Commander Pizey D.S.O. in HMS "TRITON" was to sink three German troop and supply ships in convoy on their way to Norway (10ᵗʰ April 1940). The bodies of the drowned German sailors were washed up on Marstrand.

It was blowing hard outside and despite the steadying influence of the sails we rolled abominably. Course was altered off the Skaw for Kristiansand and we set our teeth for a bad night. One moment "NAROMIS" would be planing on the top of a great wave, the next she would be slewing round and almost broaching to, then back again on course and racing forward on a surge of foam. The crew was not feeling very happy by suppertime and comforted themselves with roast potatoes. These are cheering things at sea, if you have the luxury of an oven that does not stand on its head in a seaway. They are easy to prepare, warming and good for the *mal de mer*. Although both Mike and Jock were ill, the watch bill was carried out as arranged. Indeed the latter declared afterwards, rather vulgarly no doubt, that it was the best cat he'd had in ages.

Sunday August 27th 1939

WHEN AT LAST the thin veils of dawn came, we found ourselves off Kristiansand Fjord in a confused sea. To add to the delights of daybreak, rain was falling and the watch below was called up to help get the sails off her – a miserable job to turn out of the restless bunk, pull on a sweater and shiver your way on deck, feeling tired and faintly seasick, to get down a soaking mainsail. All the halliards had tightened up and it was almost impossible to get them off the cleats. Meanwhile the boat does her best to buck you overboard. By this time your fingers and toes have lost their common feeling and you begin to think that the time has come to write home to Mother and explain that this ship's not what you thought it was and would she sell the pig at once and buy you out.

Sunday in Kristiansand was a very quiet day. As soon as we had made fast everyone turned in again for a couple of hours. By eight o'clock the usual collection of wise men and boys had arrived and remained in pretty constant attendance all the forenoon. Skipper was the first to emerge and reported that the little boys tried to get pennies out of him. Once most of the little town had come to have a look at us we decided to return the compliment and have a look at them. But there was nothing doing at all in the town and, try as we would, we couldn't buy anything. The town is built compactly and all the streets of wooden houses are straight and cross each other at right angles. The church is in the centre. The surrounding hills

Kristiansand, Norway

seemed to have cast a spell over the small township or perhaps it was the rain that made it such a sober scene.

The Customs Officer-cum-Chief of Police came on board at noon. He was a nice chap with very blue eyes: "We are glad to have ze Englesman here and not ze Deutchman from Tykesland. We have ze guns on ze cliff for ze Deutchman!" They used these guns with good effect some eight months later.

"Tykesland" amused the Skipper and we laughed a lot about it afterwards. There was no doubt which side these people were on – it was almost worth the threat of war to be so popular. "Hitler is finished!" "England must kill this monster" etc etc. However this somewhat pathetic faith in our ability to swiftly restore peace made us all feel rather bogus. How good it will be when Britain is strong again, virile and well-respected by virtue of hard work and enterprise.

We left after lunch and immediately met some colossal seas. Fortunately it was merely a question of steaming up one side and down the other – they were quite harmless. I can't think what caused them because the water was very deep, there was no tide to speak of and no more than a force 4 wind. Once we were well clear of the coast we headed due west for the South Katland light. Our destination was the little town of Farsund. We had picked this place because it was the most westerly port with a Shell oil depot. Skipper had a most excellent means of getting fuel oil supplies without the bother of foreign currency; simply a chit authorising him to be supplied in any port with Shell tanks and the total would be settled at the end of the voyage.

Presently, after picking up the S. Katland, we turned in towards the "skjaergarre" (skerries) where we thought Farsund Fjord should be. At first it looked like an unbroken line of bare rocks, hundreds of feet high. Gradually, as we threaded through the islands, the fjord revealed itself. The water became smoother and

"The sun had set..." Norway

we looked forward to discovering what sort of place we had picked for our jumping off point. It exceeded our best expectations. The sun had set and its red glow lit up a belt of cumulus clouds to the east. At the same time the west side of the fjord was silhouetted against the luminous sky, its pine trees and little wooden houses as sharp as knives. A lighted beacon blinked at us on the starboard bow and soon we were surrounded by walls of rock. I couldn't help wondering why the severe rock tolerated the little houses dotted over it, why it didn't shrug its shoulders and let them fall into the sea.

"NAROMIS" rounded a bend and behold Farsund was before it. It was quite enchanting; wooden houses clustered on the hill side and a tiny kirke half way up. The background was pine trees and mountains and the air was delicious with the smell of the warm pines. Lights danced on the water and it seemed unreal and like stage scenery.

We made fast to the quay which also seemed to be the main street. The usual crowd assembled and the small boys even ventured on deck, pressing their little noses to the wheelhouse as they would a sweet shop. The ship's company proceeded ashore as soon as possible to taste the local "Øl". There are no pubs in Norway and it's necessary to go to the shop where Mother gets her bread. The one we went to was rather fly-blown and the beer (or oil as we christened it) was gassy. Nevertheless we got down to it with a will, imagining we were seated beside the fire in the "Green Man" or the "Butt & Oyster" or wherever we would and that the glass in front of us was really a mug of old and mild.

A tiny "dock" at Farsund, Norway

Over the rooftops, Farsund, Norway

Chapter Ten: Farsund

Monday August 28th 1939

WE ONLY stayed in Farsund twenty-four hours but it is such a delightful spot that it deserves some description. The town is situated just far enough from the sea to be protected from the swell and near enough for easy access. It was built almost entirely at the beginning of the last century and the builders picked a glorious site where the fjord splits into two arms, each of which runs some ten miles further inland.

There was no half measure here. The people's very existence is the sea. Little agriculture can be carried out in the surrounding mountainous and barren country and there are no industries. The largest building in the town is the navigation school and I think that everyone here must own a boat or have an interest in a ship of some kind. There were dozens of small fishing boats (*skjektes*) 18' long, double-ended, which sat lightly on the water like a dory. These were kept at the end of long poles stuck out from gardens or moored in miniature docks. These little docks, not more than ten metres long and about eight wide, were connected to the fjord by a narrow entrance. The boats were, to the Farsunders, what a bicycle is to an Englishman and they cost, on the average, less. They are mass-produced on the neighbouring ports of Hardanger and Arendal and sell for about seventy five kroner. Children are brought up to manage these craft in the fjords and the *skjaergarre* almost before they can read.

Fishing craft are not however the main stay of this tiny port. The population is supposed to own more shipping tonnage per head than any community in the world; this is said to be more than eighty tons for every man woman and child in Farsund! I have not been able to confirm this so we will leave it at that. My informant was very proud of Norway's mercantile marine: "We are only a small nation of seven millions but we are the third maritime nation in the world". The navigation school in this town of 1400 people was for twenty captains and thirty mates.

After lunch Mike and I took the dinghy up the fjord with the idea of bathing but the scenery was so enchanting that we went on and on. The rocks towered 1500' above us, sometimes sheer into the water, other times smothered with stunted trees – mountain ash, silver spruce and conifers. The water was coal black but gradually it became shallower and the gorge narrowed. We were a bit doubtful whether we should be able to get out at the other end but we held on in hope. We passed under two very small bridges with the water only a few inches deep but the 9' dinghy managed it and presently we had the satisfaction of reaching the left arm of the main fjord instead of going back the way we had come.

When we arrived back at the ship we found she had been topped up with fuel and a large drum of diesel oil was being lowered down the forehatch at great peril to those concerned. Naturally it landed on someone's foot – the Skipper's – but he was able to bear this discomfort as it was his artificial one. He was wounded in the last war and his leg had been removed. This disability had not the slightest effect on his activities throughout the cruise – in fact I think he did more than his share of the work and got more enjoyment out of the trip than anyone. Skips was old enough to be everybody's father yet sometimes it seemed he was far and away the youngest member of the party and was a bit of a responsibility.

Well, the drum was safely stowed, the dinghy hoisted, hands shaken and we were off for Scotland.

Farsund, Norway

The last of Norway

Chapter Eleven: North of Dogger

Tuesday 29ᵗʰ August 1939

A COMPARATIVELY long passage in a motor-craft can be incredibly long and wearisome. The lively jig of these shallow draft boats accompanied by the incessant vibration of the engines is the price you have to pay for going foreign. A sailing boat is different. It is born to the sea and understands it, rides the waves with an easier motion than the power yacht that is driven from A to B by the lord knows how many horsepower. On the other hand we should not have covered one half of the distance we managed during these three weeks in a sailing boat and great praise is therefore due to "NAROMIS" whom I regard as a queen among motor-cruisers. I am equally convinced that the owners of "FALCON", "SVAAP" and "FIRECREST" would have qualified for the 'bin' if there had been clattering machines below instead of sails aloft.

The leg over from Norway to Aberdeen was not notable for anything except its discomfort. I lost count of time in the endless succession of watches; two hours on, three hours off, trying oh so hard to get some sleep. The supply of Calor gas ran out soon after we set off so we were without anything hot. We sighted absolutely nothing save a drifter off the Naze on the first night and a momentary glimpse of a shark two days later. We had had high hopes of sighting some of our cruisers which were reported to be in the vicinity by people ashore at both Kristiansand and Farsund but our hopes were doomed to disappointment. The fishing fleets were all in port by Government order and we were very much alone. The night watches were the dreariest with the boat plunging into a stiff head sea and nothing to do except watch

86

the racing water with the light of a baleful moon on the streaming foredeck and wondering whether you could be sick or not.

Wednesday 30th August 1939

IT WAS with relief therefore that I turned out early on the Wednesday morning to find that Bill had made an excellent landfall and by a quarter to eight the lighthouse on Girdle Ness was in view. By nine we had made fast in Aberdeen and the Customs were on board. Everyone in the Granite City was very kind to us and I felt lucky to change my Danish money back into sterling because the breath of the forthcoming war was in everybody's face. Perhaps it was this that made them so extraordinarily helpful. I saw it again as soon as we landed at Grimsby and later when I travelled to join my ship. It was a widespread feeling of unity between all sorts of people. I saw for instance a City business man on the train to London accepting a bite of corned beef from a soldier's 'iron ration' stuck on the end of a knife – a thing that would not have been offered a month ago and certainly not accepted!

Aberdeen

Chapter Twelve: The Last Lap

Wednesday August 30th1939

WE HAD not been in Aberdeen long before we found and employed a couple of engineers to give the Dormans the once-over. They breed engineers in Aberdeen and there cannot be many British merchant vessels without an Aberdonian in the engine room. The engineers had completed their task by the late afternoon and before nightfall we were heading south. The night was fine and we picked up the buoys and lights across the inky water without difficulty. I turned in off May Island (Firth of Forth) and awoke to find us passing the Northumberland coast.

Thursday August 31st 1939

"NAROMIS" PLUGGED south at her best speed all Thursday only easing down to listen to the news bulletins. It became increasingly apparent that it was a race whether we should reach Ramsgate before the war was declared. Everyone was speculating what role they would take: Skipper was for handing "NAROMIS" over to the Admiralty at the first opportunity to be a tender or a harbour defence craft. He hoped then to be taken on with her as a Sub-Lieut, RNVR. Bill and I had put our names down some months ago for the RNVSR – he as a future deck officer and I, through the fault of my eyes, as a 'pusser'. Jock was a L/Corporal in the territorials and was fretting because his company was supposed to guard the Law Courts and the wireless was not reassuring about the calling up of reserves. I must say I was a bit uneasy myself. I could remember the words on the sheet of paper informing me that I was enrolled in the Supplementary Reserve: "Gentlemen" (gentlemen, mark you!) "will only be called up in the event of an

Naromis *ashore*

emergency". This was looking uncommonly like one. Mike was due to finish his last few terms as a medical student and was undecided what to do until he got his degree.

Friday September 1ˢᵗ 1939
OUR SECOND night at sea passed without incident but dawn found the visibility very reduced, to about one and a half miles. We reckoned we were somewhere between Flamborough head and Spurn Point and the morning watch had been expecting to pick up the Spurn L.V. At about five thirty the fog (for fog it had developed into) thickened and the horn was brought into action. It sounded four times and then turned into something between a squeak and a raspberry and was consequently discarded.

At seven o'clock we thought we would be able to get out of the way of the steamer track and sneak round Spurn Point into the Humber if we turned ninety degrees and closed the coast. We crept in, engines slow and the lead working for its living. Suddenly Bill called out "Three fathoms!" It shoaled rapidly ... two and a half ... two... and, before Skipper who was at the helm, could take any action we were aground. The dinghy was over the side in record time and both the kedge and bower anchors out. It was no use; we were hard on and the tide was falling.

We relaxed and took stock of our position. We were certainly out of the steamer track and provided the wind did not shift to the east we should be happy enough to the next tide. What puzzled us was to know what sands we were on. We could hear the waves grumbling a little way off but this gave us no clue until the veil of fog was lifted by a stray little breeze and showed us cliffs about sixty feet high! We were on the beach and presently we heard voices to confirm this.

We didn't mind going aground on a sandbank but after going hundreds of miles without mishap to land up on a Yorkshire beach was too much! Presently we were able to wade ashore and discover where we were: a place called Aldbrough Cliffs, some miles north of the Humber.

Aldbrough Cliffs was a ramshackle collection of habitations, not, I would say, a credit to Yorkshire. It had one saving grace, however, a well-built pub. It was here that we heard the news of Germany's attack on Poland and this was the first time that the phrase "German troops moved across the frontier at dawn" that was to become so well-known during the next twenty months.

At lunch a conference decided that, in view of the turn of events we would put in at Grimsby and complete the rest of our journey by train. Jock was particularly anxious about his law courts and left us there and then. At the police station he borrowed enough to buy a ticket to London and that was the last we heard of him. We were all sorry to see him go but realised that it was the best thing to do and that we should be doing likewise in a few hours.

After carrying the two anchors further towards the sea and having a few words with the local coast guard, there was really very little else to do except sit in the sloping cabin and wait for the tide. By three in the afternoon it was playing round the hull and presently the boat staggered to her feet again and rode to the warps. The wind and sea were satisfactory and the crew proceeded to get off. For the last hour or so a motor fishing boat had been standing off, crammed with men. As soon as they saw we were afloat they came in and offered to tow us off. We christened them the pirates and Skips said he would brain the first to set foot on "NAROMIS"! This was on the principle that we might be fools but we were not bloody fools to get them to assist us and then pay some huge court bill for 'salvage'.

We had some trouble getting both the anchors inboard as they had been placed far apart and buried well into the sand but at 1615 the remaining kedge gave up a stubborn resistance and

Yorkshire beach

away we went. The motor fishing boat turned north, possibly to Bridlington from whence it had come. We were glad to see the last of it because it had been watching our struggles with the anchors with satisfaction.

At the Humber L.V. we took off a pilot and proceeded to Grimsby. There, out in the stream we saw a couple of "Town" class cruisers from the 18th Cruiser Squadron, a sea-plane and a half-a-dozen or so of our latest destroyers. I was most interested as these were the first British warships I had seen with the exception of RNVR drill ships and a couple of minesweepers. I had seen some of the Dutch and a proportion of the German Naval strength so this was a happy conclusion to an interesting and satisfactory cruise.

Saturday September 2nd 1939
Mr Clutton left "NAROMIS" in the Inner Basin where she was surrounded by trawlers proudly displaying the White at their yards. The port was a hive of industry busily commissioning some ninety fishing vessels as minesweepers, A/S and patrol vessels. There was an air of urgency and as soon as we had left "NAROMIS" in capable hands, packed our bags and tidied the cabin for the last time, we boarded the London train.

There is little more to say. When I got home that evening, I found a telegram instructing me to report forthwith to Rosyth – which had been waiting for me for nine days! Next day war was declared and I was on my way north again, clad in a disgustingly new uniform. Bill followed a couple of months later and was posted to an armed yacht. (We met two and a half years later in West Africa.) "NAROMIS" herself joined the service early the next year and plows the water "somewhere on the East Coast". Mike became a Surgeon Lieutenant RNVR and we next came across each other in Newfoundland where he was based. Jock got a commission in a county regiment and it was with the deepest regret we learned that he had been lost at Dunkirk. Iris, the Skipper's daughter became a petty officer WRNS and Skipper alone sits, cursing his luck, in Leadenhall Street.

Skipper in his infant beard, Grimsby

Afterword: His Service to the State

"I know that all individuals will wish to review their own position, too, and to consider again if they have done all they can to offer their service to the State." (Neville Chamberlain, Birmingham 17 March 1939)

 PROBATIONARY TEMPORARY Paymaster Sub-Lieutenant Jones was on his way to the submarine depot ship HMS *Forth*, serving with the 2nd submarine flotilla. He was directed to Rosyth which had recently been reactivated as a major home command responsible for the east coast of Scotland and north-east England down to Flamborough Head and (until early 1941) also the west coast of Scotland.

Rosyth itself is on the Firth of Forth; from 26 - 29 August, however, the operational submarine flotillas had deployed to their war bases in Dundee on the Firth of Tay and Blyth on the Northumberland coast. By the time *Naromis* was plugging south at her "best speed" from Aberdeen she was passing the places where Jones should have been. HMS *Forth*, a modern, purpose-built depot ship launched on the Clyde in 1938, was in Dundee. The 2nd submarine flotilla would soon be patrolling the southwest and south coast of Norway, the Skagerrak, the Kattegat, the Skaw, Heligoland Bight, the Texel – the sea areas from which *Naromis* had so recently returned. Some members of the flotilla were already at work. As *Naromis* had crossed from Farsund to Aberdeen her crew had felt that the seas were empty. This was possibly deceptive. S-class submarine HMS *Seahorse* had already been in her position south west of Stavanger from 24 August when Temporary Paymaster Jones was sightseeing in Elsinore. On 5 September she was bombed in error by a British aircraft and returned to HMS *Forth* for repair.

Submarines typically went on war patrol for a fortnight at a time before returning to be docked and replenished. *Seahorse* was in and out of HMS *Forth's* care for the first months of war until her fourth war patrol when she moved to Blyth, carried out two more patrols and was lost in January 1940 in the Heligoland Bight. HMS *Spearfish*, her sister ship, had also been patrolling the Norwegian coast from late August 1939. In September, however, she was so badly damaged off the west coast of Denmark that she spent almost six months in Rosyth dockyard being repaired. She was back on patrol from late March 1940 and was torpedoed and sunk in July. There were normally five officers and thirty six ratings on each of these submarines. Being a paymaster on a submarine depot ship in 1939-1940 must have been a little like providing support services on an RAF fighter station during the Battle of Britain, never knowing if the people whose welfare was your responsibility would return from the missions you had enabled them to make. Only three of the twelve S-class boats which were in service in 1939 survived to the end of the war. All of these submarines used HMS *Forth* as one of their sources of support.

HMS Forth

And there were others. On 4 September 1939 O class submarine HMS *Oxley* set off from HMS *Forth* on her first war patrol to Norway. She had been secured next to HMS *Triton*, newly arrived from her pre-war station in Portsmouth. On 10 September, 28 miles SSW of Stavanger, HMS *Oxley* became the first submarine casualty of the war – torpedoed by HMS *Triton*. *Triton* picked up the only two survivors and returned them to base. There was of course an inquiry but *Triton* continued to work; backwards and forwards between Rosyth (or Dundee), Norway and Scapa Flow. She achieved success against the enemy in April, as Jones noticed, then she was sent to the Mediterranean in the summer of 1940. She was lost with all hands on her fifteenth war patrol in December.

Probationary Temporary Paymaster Sub-Lieutenant Jones no longer kept a diary. When his article from Boyton Dock, which had been written in June, finally appeared in the *Yachting Monthly* magazine in November 1939 it must have echoed like a voice from another, almost unrecognisable, world.

I had come to Boyton Dock at last. For years I had dreamed of this place, and until this afternoon there had always been a train or a tide to catch.

The Dock is up the Butley River a few hundred yards, lost in a world of saltings. Judging from the fine quay and warehouse it was of some importance years ago but now it is disused and solitary.

I sat down on the grass-covered quay and watched patches of green seaweed drift down with the ebb. Over the river were the woods at Gedgrave, and away to the right was Orford Castle against the sky. A piece of frayed rope dangled from a ring-bolt into its reflection, and all the world appeared to be dozing, save for the little gnats dancing over the sea lavender.

It needed little imagination to see a hoy from the London River just making up over the tide, her sails mellow in the late afternoon sun. The chart says there is a ferry here. How long since the last one crossed, since the last barge untied, since...? The river was saying something now, and as I lay in the sun I heard it murmuring to itself about boats and men.

It told of Suffolk smugglers who ran their cargoes here and then drove a flock of sheep down the sandy lane from Boyton to cover up their cart-tracks. Of how a local farmer was deprived of his schooner and his liberty for making a run too often.

The mud was uncovering now and the little streams from it seemed eager to join the sea. I stayed for a last moment and watched a tern hover and then dive into the unruffled water with a plop. As I pulled away down river a seagull screamed after me to remember, and then, in a little while, silence save for the squeak of oars. G.A.J.

The stated policy of the *Yachting Monthly*, at this stage of the war, was business as usual. Its editor, Maurice Griffiths, wrote: "Thinking, talking and particularly reading about the war can become an insidious vice. Many people have got into the habit of wasting hours every day listening to the various broadcasts of rehashed and restricted 'news', of buying edition after edition of evening papers and reading identical phrases, of discussing rumours and probabilities that no one knows anything about. It is not only a waste of time, it is unsettling and a waste of nervous energy which at this time none can well afford.

"During these long blackout evenings at home and in the periods of boredom that inevitably follow spells of activity in the Services, it is far better to occupy one's mind with continuous pleasant reading. For this the yachtsman will naturally yearn for his books of sailing and cruising and of tales of the sea. To become absorbed in the story of a well-described cruise, or in the plans of an attractive dream ship, is to preserve a calm outlook on a life that appears to have gone crazy."(*Yachting Monthly* November 1939)

Griffiths appealed for readers to keep their contributions coming. "Many of them must have stored up in the past years memories, logs or notes of successful cruises, the story of which might delight others to read."

Jack Jones, still working as an industrial designer in Birmingham, was an energetic and often controversial contributor – until he joined the RNVR early in 1941. George Jones was silent. Later in November 1939 Maurice Griffiths joined HMS *Vernon* in Portsmouth as a Temporary Lieutenant RNVR for mine-clearance duties and discovered the impossibility of combining active service with magazine editorship – or even the writing up of many "well-described cruises". In March 1940 the magazine changed its title and became *The Yachting Monthly and RNVR Journal*. It was edited, managed (and increasingly written) by Kathleen Palmer, Griffiths's former assistant, from her home in New Barnet.

"Time spent on reconnaissance is seldom wasted," was one of Jones's favourite sayings in later life and, while he had no time (or possibly inclination) to write up his three weeks on *Naromis* for *Yachting Monthly* or anyone else in 1939-1940, he took some of the photographs to his commanding officer, Captain W.D. Stephens. On 29 September Captain Stephens forwarded photographs of the *Gneisenau* and the *Konigsberg* to the Director of Naval Intelligence at the Admiralty. These had been taken just six weeks earlier in Kiel. The Director wrote back requesting "that Paymaster Lt G.A. Jones be thanked for supplying them". In April 1940 the *Konigsberg* was bombed and sunk in Bergen harbour. This was the first time in the history of war that a major cruiser had been sunk by air attack. A similar attempt in June to destroy the *Gneisenau*, the *Scharnhorst* and the *Admiral Hipper* (spotted but not photographed by *Naromis*) in Trondheim harbour failed as inadequate bombs were used. Eight out of fifteen Skua aircraft were lost in the attempt.

The *Gneisenau* was a major battleship. She was the flagship of German Vizeadmiral Marschall and on 23 November 1939 she had led the attack that destroyed the Armed Merchant Cruiser *Rawalpindi*, killing 238 men. This was a huge propaganda success for Germany but also an opportunity for the First Sea Lord, Winston

Churchill, to praise the stubborn heroism of the *Rawalpindi*'s captain, Edward Kennedy, and her crew: "They must have known that there was no chance for them but they had no thought of surrender. They fought their guns till they could be fought no more and they then – many of them – went to their deaths..." (House of Commons 27 November 1939) In the *Gneisenau*'s battlegroup when she had left Wilhemshaven on 21 November were not only her sister ship, the *Scharnhorst*, but also the cruisers *Koln* and *Leipzig* and the destroyers *Brend Von Armin*, *Karl Glaster* and *Eric Geise* – all of which (apart from the *Brend Von Armin*) had been observed from *Naromis* in August.

In this first period of his service, Jones concentrated entirely on his job. From 25 August 1939 to 30 January 1940 he was working as an assistant paymaster or, in the old style, a "pusser". In modern terms he was a logistics officer, responsible for the provision of equipment and food as well as managing money and accounts. He would have been expected to manage people too and occasionally to represent them in disciplinary procedures. "He has conducted himself to my entire satisfaction," wrote Captain Stephens. HMS *Forth* moved back from Dundee into Rosyth itself, then, in September 1940, as the theatre of war shifted, she was relocated to Holy Loch on the west coast of Scotland. Instead of Norway and the North Sea the submarines in her care were frequently ordered down to the Bay of Biscay, an increasingly perilous location as the German U-boat fleet colonised the Atlantic harbours of occupied France.

On that same day, so long ago, in June 1939 that Jones had written his wistful article for the *Yachting Monthly*, he had also recorded details of a disaster. "A ghastly accident. The submarine *Thetis* is wrecked with ninety souls on board. The stern was above water and they could not release them. Just faint tappings on the hull. Then silence. God help them inside." (3 June 1939)

Now, in the autumn of 1940, in Holy Loch, he was one of the HMS *Forth* team ready to support HMS *Thunderbolt*. *Thunderbolt* was *Thetis*, salvaged. She had been commissioned in October 1940, carried out her trials on the Clyde then left HMS *Forth* in December on her first war patrol to the Bay of Biscay. On this occasion she returned safely and was enabled to carry out two more patrols until both she and HMS *Forth* moved across the Atlantic to Halifax, Nova Scotia. *Thunderbolt*'s subsequent career was eventful. She travelled thousands of miles between different war zones until she was finally lost on 14 March 1943 off Cape St Vito, Sicily.

With the entire continental coast from north Norway to Finisterre in enemy hands the strategic priorities for the Navy in the autumn of 1940 were the defence of Britain against invasion and the increasingly significant Battle of the Atlantic. Britain's continued existence depended on the delivery of supplies from all over the world by sea. Merchant ships were immediately organised into convoys but were horribly vulnerable to attack by German U-boats. From the late summer of 1940 these U-boats were able to operate from bases on the west coast of Occupied France and were organised into lethally effective "wolf-packs". There were surface raiders too and Allied casualties were high, both amongst the merchant ships, their escorts and those lone submarines sent out on their war patrols. In January 1940 HMS *Forth* moved to the convoy port of Halifax to support the escort system. Jones was now working as a cypher officer and Captain Stephens had become deputy director of naval intelligence.

The Battle of the Atlantic was grim, protracted and strategically crucial (Churchill later described it as the only thing that had really worried him during the course of the war). Three months after HMS *Forth*'s arrival in Halifax, Jones persuaded his new captain, G. C. P. Menzies, to write a letter to the admiral in charge of submarines pleading the case of "many keen seamen [who] have been compelled through poor eyesight to join the service as officers of the accountant branch of either the RNR or the RNVR". These men could still be sent to sea: "It is suggested that such officers could be employed to advantage as Liaison Officers in Allied Submarines where it would not be essential for them to have technical knowledge, but where their knowledge of cypher would be particularly valuable." (13 April 1941)

The reply from the Admiral was blunt. There was "no requirement" for the officers referred to in paragraph one (ie those, like Jones, with defective eyesight who had joined the accountant branch). A number of RNVR "executive officers" (those passed fit for active duties) had already volunteered and were being trained. (11 May 1941) The division between the accountant and executive branches of the service seemed unbridgeable. Jones had no option but to continue with the job he had been given. He was promoted to Lieutenant and Captain Menzies later commended him as "a very able and energetic officer who has been of great service to the flotilla". Jones began to do more than his regular duties demanded. He requisitioned a motor cutter and undertook a survey of the Halifax harbour entrance: he also offered various recommendations for improving the protection of convoys and modifying the escape hatch design in submarines. All his suggestions were politely acknowledged – and rejected.

When HMS *Forth* moved on again in the autumn of 1941 to St John's, Newfoundland, Jones appears to have begun to enjoy his unsought leisure. He made friends ashore, went sailing – including a memorable trip in a Grand Banks Schooner – and finally wrote down his memories of the three weeks in *Naromis*, so long ago. This may have been prompted by a chance meeting with his fellow crew-member Mike, now an RNVR surgeon. Jones also collected a further sixty-one photographs "giving views of beaches, bridges, important landmarks and harbours in Norway, Sweden, Denmark, North Germany and Holland" and sent them to Naval Intelligence. (23 December 1941) These photographs, it seems, were accepted as potentially useful. When Jones asked for their return, many months

Sailing a Grand Banks schooner

later, he was informed that they had all been mounted and filed, though copies could be made available. (18 September 1942)

By this time he was clearly beginning to wonder whether the account might one day make a book and wrote to *Yachting Monthly's* Kathleen Palmer for advice. Her reply was encouraging and also interesting as it displays some of the tact she brought to her management of *The RNVR Journal* at this time: "Meanwhile I have heard from Jack who you no doubt have heard was wounded in the Dieppe raid. But his letter was cheerful and he expected to be returning to service quite soon. When I did not hear from you, I wrote to your mother, whose address Jack had given me, and she wrote and told me he was in hospital. I did not write to her until it was obvious you were a very long way away, just in case the news was bad and I should cause her extra distress. (2 October 1942)

She made several helpful suggestions concerning possible publishers but there's no evidence that Jones made any attempt to contact them. He was by now stationed in West Africa.

HMS *Forth* had returned home for a refit in November 1941. Jones remembered later that he had been hoping for some home leave and also, perhaps, a posting to a ship on more active service.

On my return from America in November 1941, the ship, my dear old Forth, did a refit in Rosyth. We left there just after Christmas and proceeded to the Clyde, with two destroyers and the A/A cruiser Curacao as escort. As the fleet turned into the Pentland Firth, two Spitfires gambolled overhead, flirting, chasing each other's tails, diving, rolling, climbing, a pure delight to watch. They were our escort too. The sun came out that morning and the low snow-covered hills of Thursoe and Orkney were covered with light.

Many of the Wardroom were expecting to leave the ship. I was one. I had been aboard for more than two years and there was an air of expectancy, officers discussing where they would like to go and how they were going up to the Admiralty to try and fix it with someone they knew. [...] Soon after our arrival in Holy Loch the half yearly promotions to Cmdr came out. It was New Year's Eve: the Captain was leaving. All these things called for a party. The Wardroom dined the Captain and "Tubby" Linton who was later to win the V.C. He was the fourth V.C. to dine in Forth's Wardroom — Myers, Wanklyn and Roberts had gone before. It was my last Guest Night in my first ship and quite a memorable one too. Next morning I said goodbye to my admirable Captain G.C.P. Menzies. A fine captain gifted with great vision and energy. I hoped to go with him to his next appointment.

In fact Jones was sent on to another submarine depot ship, HMS *Titania*, to act as interim Captain's Secretary for Commander H.R. Conway.

I was shanghaied to Titania to assist in the turnover from the 2ⁿᵈ to the 3ʳᵈ Submarine flotilla. Of "Tights" I'll say only a couple of lines. Old, ugly and supremely uncomfortable and inefficient in many ways, she was the happiest ship I've been in. She has been in many places and been many submarines' depot ship. In two wars submariners have lived in her for hard work and parties and have gone out on patrol from her side. She is one of the oldest serving ships in this war, and one of the grandest.

He was still hoping for something different.

On leaving Tights safely in dock in Glasgow, I went on leave. On passing through London I took it upon myself to pay my respects to the P.D.G (Paymaster Director General) only to learn that I had been appointed to another ship that was due to leave the U.K within the week. Her name was Philoctetes. A new Dido class cruiser perhaps...? Er, no, not exactly. A depot ship. Oh Lord! Not another depot ship. Yes, and going either to the Eastern Fleet or to West Africa. Four days leave. A quick run round to say goodbye. I went to Sheerness to see my brother who was in command of an M/L there. I came to Newney I remember and saw them for a few brief hours. The surrounding fields were pockmarked by bomb craters, the windows for the most part blown out, ceilings were down.

These were not the only changes Jones would have noticed on this tantalisingly brief leave. Aunts Georgie and Margaret were long gone from Fleet House and living in Long Melford. The Willises had let out Grafton Manor house and moved into the Tithe Barn. The Severn Sailing Club was laid up and would remain largely forgotten until the 1960s. His brother Jack, commanding HDML (Harbour Defence Motor Launch) 1024, had already suffered four months in hospital following an underwater explosion. *Hustler,* however, was in safe hands, being faithfully looked after by Jimmy Quantrill at Waldringfield. This was Jones's first trip home since his single overnight stay on return from *Naromis* on 2 September 1939. He would not be back for another two years. "My dear Jones," wrote G.C.P Menzies (now promoted from Captain to Commodore) "I hear

you were quickly whipped off into an active job [...] I am sorry we
cannot be together again." (HMS *Orion* 28 January 1942)

*On the 14ᵗʰ January [1942] I joined Philoctetes at Greenock and
we sailed on 17ᵗʰ at midnight. "Phil" was a converted merchant liner
late of the Alfred Holt line. In her day – that is the 1920s – she was the
largest merchant ship and capable of carrying over 20,000 tons of cargo.
Converted in 1941 by Harland and Wolff's of Belfast, she was designed
to look after two modern destroyer flotillas. Heavy and light machine shops,
a foundry, torpedo and ordnance workshops, bakery, store rooms for flour,
provisions, clothes, naval stores and altogether hundreds of items necessary
to repair, provision and re-equip perhaps a score of escort vessels and their
ships' companies. In point of fact we were looking after nearly five score at
Freetown when the Mediterranean was closed and the West Africa Station
became strategically so important.*

*We sailed some hours after the O.S. convoys which we were to join. For
two days we hunted for them off the north coast of Ireland and finally
put in at Loch Foyle to await an escort. This was soon forthcoming and*

HMS Philoctetes

we put to sea again. Impression: the wonderful green fields, stone walls and clearness of Donegal. We joined the convoy and for the next week went through some shocking weather. The convoy speed was at one time down to four and a half knots but the ships kept together and plugged south till the weather moderated and the day's runs passed the 200-a-day mark.

We sailed out of the winter into the sunshine, out of the raging spume-blown North Atlantic into moderate seas, clear blue, deeper than the conscious mind could allow, seas with sharks and flying fish, barracuda and turtles.

On the voyage out there was little work for me to do. There were the not-too-strenuous cypher watches, store-room and adjacent compartment rounds for me and the task of getting to know a large Accountant Division. [...] There were dawn and dusk action stations and you almost prayed that something would happen. [...] When off-watch we slept or took a turn on deck, played cards, drank horses-necks, yarned, yawned and waited for the next meal. One of our passengers, a Brigadier who had been on the coast for many tours, gave a lecture to the troops about what to expect and how to behave in West Africa. He talked about the venomous black and green mambas, jiggers, sun helmets, malaria, venereal disease and the Africans. There was much speculation as whether we would have to go to Las Palmas for coal ("Phil" was coal-burning) or whether we could make Bathurst in the Gambia. We made the Gambia with only a few tons left.

I cannot easily forget my first sight of Africa. We arrived off the mouth of the Gambia River early in February – the 6th I think – and, after picking up a pilot, moved up to the anchorages off Bathurst. The town is built on an island and is very attractive viewed from the river. Flooded with sunlight, white surf from the Atlantic to seaward, sand beaches merging into mangrove swamps up the river. Native canoes under sail and paddle, industriously going nowhere, palm trees, white walled houses with hibiscus in their gardens, crowds of natives with clothes in a dozen colours.

Soon after the hook was down we felt the weight of the sun. The ship's company at last had reason to change into tropical uniform. A few hardy officers had made it a few days before arrival at Bathurst but had been forced by cold knees and arms to change into blue-uniform again.

"Away, pinnace's crew!" Captain going ashore to make arrangements for the burial of a stoker who had died the night before due to an accident. I was able to go ashore with the paymaster commander to change money for the ship's company. The pinnaces were new, the coxswain was new, so we flashed ashore at very great speed with a great white wake astern. Exiting with sunlight on the waves, a cloudless sky and a new continent ashore. Land after nearly three weeks at sea. Achievement and a beginning of new things.

HMS *Philoctetes* had been posted to Freetown in Sierra Leone, whose importance as a base for convoy escorts rapidly increased. When *Philoctetes* arrived she became the depot ship for the 18th Destroyer Flotilla comprising two sloops and twenty four corvettes and this number continued to grow during the period Jones was there. According to Richard Woodman, Freetown was not a popular posting. He quotes a corvette officer as saying: "We swelter in godawful heat and everyone thinks you're a cissy if you don't have a bout of malaria every fortnight … the only things free in Freetown are sweat and syphilis." (*The Real Cruel Sea* p.306) Another veteran recalled that HMS *Philoctetes* was nicknamed "flock of fleas" because of her poor conditions. (http://www.harry-tates.org.uk/veteranstales15.htm)

There is no record of Jones complaining. On the voyage out and for his first eight months in Freetown he was serving once again as a Temporary Paymaster Lieutenant. In April 1942, two months after his arrival, he submitted a detailed analysis of the current harbour defences with suggestions for additional precautions that might usefully be taken. More ideas followed in October, as well as a list of practical suggestions in September for more effective tactics to ensure enemy U-boats were captured intact; eg "To supplement the International Code, and to assist any non-German or non-Italian speaking officers in charge of boarding parties, a few phrases such as 'If the submarine

GA Jones, Captain's Secretary
HMS Philoctetes 1943

Ned Guinness

is scuttled you will not be saved', 'All men fall in on deck', 'Where is the Engineer Officer?' printed on a card with their phonetic equivalent and issued in O.U. 5210 (Boarding Officers packet) should prove helpful." (20 September 1942) His first Captain (R. St V. Sherbrooke) recommended him for a permanent commission, adding "He is keen, a good leader and full of initiative and is always glad to undertake any work in or outside his department that comes along." (1 October 1942)

Jones now had the status of Qualified Officer and was given additional responsibility as Second Account Officer, Account Divisional Officer and Captain's Secretary in the Freetown Escort Force. This promotion was clearly a success. Various of his good ideas appeared to have been acted on and a confidential report written after a convivial evening with a group of young French Naval Officers was regarded as sufficiently perceptive to be passed upwards from *Philoctetes*'s Captain Henderson to the Flag Officer Commanding West Africa. When not on duty Jones took opportunities to explore the surrounding area and meet some of the people who lived there. His scrap book contains pages of stamps, photographs of people and places, souvenirs from expeditions which were frequently undertaken with his immediate superior, Captain 'Ned' (Edward Douglas) Guinness RNR. When possible they would take *Moira*, "a fat, stubby, little Scottish fishing boat", and go exploring up river and trawling for strange tropical fish.

Guinness, an Irish aristocrat, called Jones 'My dear George' and wrote him a long and thoughtful letter on his voyage home to the UK reflecting on what had made their working partnership on *Philoctetes* so special. "The job – my first chief's appointment – gave me the opportunity, for which I had always longed, of putting into practice my theory that to get the best out of your staff you must reduce to a minimum detailed orders of what they should or should not do. Voluminous orders kill enterprise and tend to prevent men thinking for themselves; they kill initiative, without which any organisation is moribund. My immediate superiors have always held the opposite theory..." (HMS *Sennen*, February 1943) Elsewhere Guinness described Jones as "outstanding" and recommended him for promotion to Lieutenant Commander even though, aged twenty-five, he was officially too young. His recommendation was supported by Captain Henderson, Captain of the Freetown Escort Force, who pointed out that Lieutenant Jones had already been fulfilling this role for nine months by default.

During the autumn of 1943 Jones began to find it hard to summon his usual enthusiasm for work and the ship's surgeon diagnosed him as suffering from general debility. "I am of the opinion that, observing he has already completed twenty two months service on this station, he should be sent home as soon as possible to obviate any further deterioration in his health." (27 November 1943) There was little delay and Jones travelled back to England on board Flower-class corvette HMS *Stonecrop*. By co-incidence this was the ship which, in April, had sunk U-124, Germany's highest scoring U-boat, together with the sloop HMS *Black Swan*. On 9 November *Black Swan*'s Acting Temporary Lieutenant Commander William

Archibald Fuller RNVR, "Bill" from *Naromis*, had been awarded the Distinguished Service Cross for his part in the action. Jones would never be a hero like Bill, like Edward Kennedy or Maurice Griffiths, like the VC's who had dined in *Forth's* ward room and all those gallant submariners risking their lives on every war patrol – or like his own brother Jack who, seriously wounded, had brought his RML (Rescue Motor Launch) safely back from the Dieppe Raid in April 1943 with himself strapped to the wheel as there was no one else on board able to steer.

Jones was unequivocally glad to be home and this time he was allowed six weeks leave before taking up his new duties at HMS *Badger*, Harwich.

One morning as I lay abed at Newney [the family farm in Essex] listening to the silence and the rooks and starlings and cows it came to me that these things had been missing for so long as to be strangers. Cheap, common ordinaries of no par value, these sounds would have remade the world for many of the thousands of Englishmen in West Africa or for that matter the millions away from home – in India and Ascension Island, in Labradour or in the prison camps of Siam.

RN Club at Harwich 1945

Jones served two more years from February 1944 to March 1946. In Harwich he was involved in the rigorously secret preparations for the Normandy Landings. Early in the morning of 6 June, Force L sailing groups 1 and 2 left Harwich Harbour. They comprised sixty-five major landing craft and ships, escorted by destroyers, corvettes, anti-submarine trawlers, motor launches and minesweepers. It was a triumph of logistics as well as a platform for heroism and, though there could never be parity of esteem between those who were actively risking their lives and those who remained behind, there were signs that the divisions within the service were beginning to break down. When Jones was finally promoted to Lieutenant Commander, in July 1945, he no longer had to qualify this with the term "paymaster". He was now Temporary Lieutenant Commander (S) G.A. Jones RNVR, strongly recommended for accelerated promotion and for transfer onto the permanent list.

J.P. Foynes's invaluable book *The Battle of the East Coast 1939-1945* explains how the seaward end of the Western Front shifted to the Low Countries after the success of the Normandy landings. The southern North Sea, which had been quiet for many months, was once again the location for final desperate activity by enemy E-boats and small U-boats. The destroyers were back in Harwich and the need for mine-sweeping was intense. Even after VE day when some beaches were re-opened to the public and some pleasure sailing permitted on inland waters there was much to be done. The German E-boat commanders had been obliged to hand over their mine-laying charts at a special ceremony in Harwich on 13 May 1945 and a huge clearance operation was then undertaken, headed by Jones's new Captain T.W. Marsh. "There were ten times as many mines (of both sides) to be swept in peace time as were swept throughout the war." (*Battle of the East Coast* p373)

Jones remained in service until the spring of 1946. Once again his commendations were glowing. "He has carried out a most difficult duty efficiently and cheerfully. He is conscientious, reliable and methodical. A keen boat sailor, a good mixer and one who takes part in all the social activities of the base." (Captain T.W. Marsh 16 January 1946) He was released in March with the war service rank of Lieutenant Commander and retained on the RNVR list. He was clear however where his heart lay.

I came to a reassuring conclusion when I was at Waldringfield. I've lost faith in most of the things I used to have as ideals or fancies. They've dulled and don't fire me anymore. But one thing still retains its fascination – mystery if you like – and that is the Deben. To see it as I left it at eight o'clock last night with the sun setting low in the west lighting up the fresh spring green of trees over Stonor Point and the Tips, a single sailing ship beating down the Bowships on the last of the ebb. To hear the familiar sound of a tractor putting in some overtime across the estuary at Shottisham, the occasional call of a curlew or redstart on the saltings, then I know there is nothing I want more than to get back to this part of Suffolk.

It had been a long time since that summer of 1939 when he left for *Naromis* and the Baltic.

Jimmy Quantrill and Hustler *at Waldringfield*

Appendix One:
"Time Spent on Reconnaissance"

COPY NEG N 4190

COPY NEG N 4191

COPY NEG N 4195

COPY NEG N 4187

Reproduced here is the list of photographs with George Jones sent to Naval Intelligence in December 1941 when his ship, HMS *Forth*, was back in the U.K. for refit, before he left her for HMS *Titania*.

The nine photographs of merchant ships reproduced here were returned to him in December 1942 mounted and with reference numbers not in his handwriting. None of the photographs of seamarks and places listed here are among Jones's papers now. Either they were retained or they have simply been lost.

The whole business seems odd. This list of photographs is clearly presented as a reconnaissance list, aids for identification if expeditions were being made to these enemy-occupied countries. Is that why they were taken in the first place? Even for a cruising yachtsman they are not quite the usual summer

COPY NEG N 4193

COPY NEG N 4188

COPY NEG N 4192

COPY NEG N 4189

holiday snaps. They seem to confirm that there was an aspect of *Naromis*'s August 1939 expedition that was consciously intended to be of assistance to the coming war. Then why did Jones not send them earlier? Because he was busy? The first two photographs were forwarded by Captain Stephens from HMS *Forth* to Naval Intelligence in September 1939, more than two years previously – and Captain Stephens's next posting was in Intelligence. If he'd seen the others and thought they mattered presumably he would have allowed Jones some time to organise a list and possibly write an explanatory letter? These were the waters in which Captain Stephens's submarines were operating.

Also, why was it Jones, possibly the youngest member of the crew, who was responsible– not Bill Fuller, for instance? Fuller seems to be the most knowledgeable and the driving force (apart from the Skipper) and I have assumed he was the person who took the photos of the *Gneisenau* and the *Konigsberg*. Yet it was Jones who had them in his possession at Rosyth. Perhaps because he was the first to be called up for duty? Who took the rest of the photographs? Jones clearly identifies this list as his. Did all of them carry cameras? Was it significant that Jones had met Mike in Nova Scotia?

All I can do here is present the evidence. This is the list that my father kept with his papers.

Editor's Note: The most likely reason that George's photographs of the Scandinavian coastline, seamarks, etc were not sent to Naval Intelligence in September 1939 at the same time as those of the warships, *Konigsburg* and *Gneisenau*, was that at that point the Admiralty would not have been interested in such information. In *Ian Fleming's Commandos* (Faber 2011) Nicholas Rankin reveals that the intelligence file on Norway at the time landings were attempted in April 1940 was completely empty. It was thanks to the efforts of Fleming's boss Admiral John Godfrey (the original of "M") that the Inter-Services Topographical Department was set up later that year. George's letter with his photographs (written in 1941) explains he is sending them in response to *Weekly Intelligence Report no 80*, a briefing sheet for which Fleming was partially responsible.

Julia Jones, February 2017

ENCLOSURE TO TEMPORARY PAYMASTER LIEUTENANT G.A. JONES, RNVR'S LETTER DATED 23 DECEMBER, 1941

SUMMARY OF PHOTOGRAPHS
NORWAY
1. Aerial view of Farsund.
2. Bridge connecting Farsund with Austad.
3. Bridge connecting Farsund with Austad.
4. View of Farsund (Navigation School).
5. View of Farsund from North.
6. Approaches to Farsund through Skerriaguard.
7. Approaches to Farsund 58° 05'N 06° 50'E
7a Off Lister, near Farsund.
8. Farsund Fjord – beyond bridges.
9. Map and bridges about Farsund.

SWEDEN
10. Beacon in Hake Fjord or Vinga Sound, Gothenburg.
11. Beacon in Hake Fjord or Vinga Sound, Gothenburg.
11a Beacon in Rife Fjord, Gothenburg.
12. Naval base, Gothenburg.
13. Naval base, Gothenburg, submarines alongside.
14. Naval base, Gothenburg.
15. Fullen Light 56° 17'N 12° 35'E
16. Buoy in Approaches to Malmo.
17. Buoy in Approaches to Malmo.
18. Time ball at Malmo.

DENMARK
19. Burmeister and Wain's Yard, Copenhagen.
20. Elsinore, indicating position of Shipyard.
21. Orehoved, Falster.

GERMANY

HOLLAND

MERCHANT SHIPS.

50. German, possibly "ODER" or "LAHN"
51. Italian tanker.
52. Norwegian Tanker "BEAN".
53. Danish "KINA".
54. Danish "KRONPRINZ OLAF".
55. Swedish "FINN" (?).
56. Swedish "BALBOA" or Danish "ALSIA".
57. Unidentified.
58. Unidentified.
59. Unidentified.

Sixty-one (61) photographs and pamphlets giving views of beaches, bridges, important landmarks and harbours in Norway, Sweden, Denmark, North Germany and Holland, suitably "keyed".

Appendix Two: After the War

Naromis was too small for her war service to be recorded in the reference books (as far as I have discovered). She didn't go to Dunkirk though some of her sisters did. Instead she was one of the hundreds of private yachts working as tenders, as harbour defence

Naromis *as MY* Bayeed

patrol craft, as air sea rescue vessels or on "miscellaneous services". Sometime after the war her name was changed to MY *Bayeed.* She retired to the Mediterranean and was still registered in Gibraltar in 1999.

George Jones and his brother Jack settled back in Waldringfield. Jack and their mother, Edith, bought the Old Maltings – a tall Georgian house with views of the boatyard and the river. There Jack commenced his career as a significant post-war yacht designer (see *Yachting Monthly* January 2016, *Classic Sailor* December 2015).

George did not join with them in the house purchase. Instead he made use of the stables at the back of the Old Maltings to establish his East Coast Yacht Agency ("Easy Cosy") with an RNVR friend, Anthony Daniels. This was soon successful and the office moved to Quay Street, Woodbridge – just a few miles further up the Deben. George and Jack worked closely together: Jack

Jack Jones

designing and surveying, George building and selling. One of his first customers was June Scott who bought the engine-less, over-canvassed, speedy *Snow Goose.* They married in 1950 and their three children Julia, Nicholas and Edward were all born in Woodbridge and introduced to sailing on the River Deben. In 1957 George and June bought Arthur Ransome's post-war designed ketch, *Peter Duck,* and kept her until after George's death in 1983.

The moment George looked longingly at the small 24' clinker-built fishing boats in Nakskov (August 19th 1939) may have been seminal. It was certainly characteristic. When the UK market became dominated by GRP in the 1970s George sold the Easy Cosy and founded Beagle Boats, building small, wooden clinker-built fishing boats designed by his brother Jack. They weren't exactly a mass-market success and George used his new-found leisure to broker the purchase and restoration of historic vessels for St Katherine's Dock in London; to raise funds for the East Coast Sail Trust (managing the Thames Sailing Barges *Thalatta* and *Sir Alan Herbert*) and take up water-colour painting. For many years he was also the Coast Notes correspondent for the *Yachting Monthly.* So perhaps he did achieve some of the ambitions that he'd played around with, aged 21, in the earlier months of 1939.

George sailing Peter Duck

Also published by Golden Duck

The Allingham series:

The Adventures of Margery Allingham Julia Jones

Cheapjack: 'being the True History of a Young Man's Adventures as a Fortune-Teller, Grafter, Knocker-Worker, and Mounted Pitcher on the Market-Places and Fairgrounds of a Modern but still Romantic England.' Philip Allingham

Fifty Years in the Fiction Factory: the Working Life of Herbert Allingham 1867-1936 Julia Jones

The Oaken Heart: the Story of an English Village at War Margery Allingham

Beloved Old Age – and What To Do About It: Margery Allingham's *The Relay* handed on to Julia Jones

The 'Strong Winds' series by Julia Jones:

The Salt-Stained Book (also available as an audio book)

A Ravelled Flag

Ghosting Home

The Lion of Sole Bay

Black Waters

Other titles:

Wild Wood Jan Needle

Keeping a Sketchbook Diary Claudia Myatt

GOLDEN DUCK

www.golden-duck.co.uk
Our titles are available to order through all good bookshops
as well as via the internet. Most titles are also available in Kindle format